From Pixels to Prose

What Video Games Taught Me About Storytelling

Nadia Oxford

Retro Game Books, LLC
San Francisco, CA
RetroGameBooks.com

ISBN 978-1-966009-03-0
First printing edition

Editor: Justin Severson
Cover art: Philip Summers
Editor-in-Chief: Brian Riggsbee

This book is dedicated to all the freako writers across history who've asked themselves, "Okay, but what was the real intent behind Judas' kiss?"

CONTENTS

Foreword

If I were to sum up the entirety of my roughly 25-year career of working in the games industry and adjacent spaces, it would be: "a comedy of errors trying to hire Nadia Oxford full-time."

I don't actually remember how I first came across Nadia's work, mainly because it happened so long ago that it nearly predates the human invention of "writing down history for preservation." Now, if someone put a gun to my head to demand that I pin down the story (terrorists have some very niche demands these days), I could probably gin up a convincing lie that it definitely happened via Live-Journal. I don't know if kids these days are aware of LiveJournal, unless they live in Russia, but once upon a time you really had to *look* to find Cyrillic text on that service. Back then, it was used by North American teens and twentysomethings to vaguepost about their annoyances or write about their meals. Like Twitter, but with no hard word cap. Back when Twitter existed.

Not sure if kids these days know what Twitter is, either, come to think of it. The world changes. But what doesn't change is the fact that Nadia has one of the most authentic writing voices I've ever come across. She has a distinct perspective, with an ability to cut to the heart of what makes a video game great. And unlike most people writing about video games, such as myself, her commentary rarely centers on the mechanics and systems of gameplay. Certainly she *can* write about those things when the assignment calls for it, but Nadia in her natural element writes about the emotional impact of games through their interplay of narrative and interactivity.

Any dork can write about how *Super Mario* plays, but Nadia has the rare ability to tell you how it *feels*. She doesn't seem to dwell on grand statements about coding and digital physics, preferring instead to place herself in the hero's big stompy shoes and explore *Super Mario* from Mario's perspective: why is he tromping through the Mushroom Kingdom yet again? Does it hurt when he eats a flower and starts flinging fire all over the place? Does he pay reparations to the families of the citizens he accidentally murders over the course of his adventure when he shatters the bricks that King Koopa's black magic has transformed them into? And, most importantly, what does kissing Princess Toadstool taste like? Her real name is Peach, so you'd think it would be feminine and sweet. But she's also been trapped for who knows how long in Bowser's magma-filled castle, which has to be swelteringly hot, so she probably has some f---in' gnarly dehydration breath.

Oh, right: I'd be remiss if I didn't mention that Nadia's distinct perspective frequently involves cusses and innuendos. About video games. But, unlike most people who write rude things about video games, that rudeness is neither the entire point nor a crutch to compensate for a lack of substance. I think the little blips of bawdiness are just the earnest product of a slightly dirty mind, honestly. Nadia keeping it real. And grounded: let's face it, when you're writing prose about the inner emotional turmoil of combat robots who don't even know how to use a calendar correctly (what kind of notation is "20XX", anyway?), you need a little realism to keep the whole thing from flying off into the realm of lah-dee-dah navel-gazing. Or whatever passes for a navel on a combat robot. Probably a USB port of some kind.

Anyway, that kind of viewpoint has always been distressingly rare in writing about video games, which is why I've been trying to figure out how to hire Nadia for years. The stupidest complications keep getting in the way, though. Dumb stuff like "she lives in Ontario and our website only hires people who can work in our San Francisco office" or "we finally have the perfect opening but I'm quitting this job and they won't let me make long-term budgetary decisions anymore." I've had to settle for bringing her into the fold as a cohost of the Retronauts podcast, where she's great, but podcasts aren't writing! Those are different disciplines altogether, Jan.

Well, the world hasn't ended yet, so it's not impossible that I might still find some way to shackle Nadia to a writing desk and make her crank out funny, poignant words about video games for 40 hours a week. Then again, maybe not. Once the world comes across this book and peers into Nadia's soul — that mysterious cauldron where thoughts about video games and emotions churn together into alchemical prose — I suspect I won't be the only one clamoring to recruit Nadia to write. All I can say is: back off, chumps. I was here first.

— Jeremy Parish

CHAPTER 1

Video Games Can Tell Stories? Since When?

"How high can you get?" - *Donkey Kong*

Every human has at least one "thing" that lights a spark and compels them to indulge themselves until they're sick, if they're allowed. I was born two weeks past my due date with a compulsion to find and absorb stories, folklore, faerie tales, and legend. I needed to hear them, read them, and watch the awkward movies assembled from their bones. I also had a compulsion to eat styrofoam, so be assured I'm not trying to make myself sound like I was a budding starchild.

Books were my favourite, especially stories by Judy Blume and books about Ramona being a chaotic shit all up and down Klickitat Street. C.S. Lewis's Narnia series had me enthralled despite starting with *The Last Battle*, the last book in the series' timeline. As a young Jew unfamiliar with the Book of Revelations, it was wild to watch a black sun descend on a frozen, broken Narnia that was promptly reborn. The symbolism meant nothing to me; as far as I knew, I'd just gone on a literary acid trip with unicorns, centaurs, and bestial false gods pre-supplied. No wonder I was hooked. When someone insists I must start a story or series from the first book/episode, I tell them I read the Narnia series backwards and loved it. This isn't math! Stories don't need no order of operations!

Movies can also tell great stories, but I admit it took time for movies to grow on me. First I had to drop my snobbish habit of automatically condemning movies as inherently inferior to the books they're based on. It was a slow journey given how badly I was gaslit by 1971's *Willy Wonka & the Chocolate Factory* as a youngster. The book has nothing resembling the tunnel scene wherein Gene Wilder shepherds a boatload of screaming kids through an LSD trip like a garish Charon. Was there a scene in the book where the kids see footage of bugs crawling out of a woman's mouth? Had I even *read* the right book? It shames me now to think there was a time when I regarded that twisted movie masterpiece with anything other than reverence. I don't deserve heaven.

I also loved stories in comic books, and in fact learned to read thanks to my dad's *MAD Magazine* collection (only the highest-quality reading content in my parents' house), my brother's *Archie* comics, and the incessant trickle of *Beano* comics that invariably makes its way from overseas if you have so much as one relative in the United Kingdom.

The itch to write inevitably followed my reading sessions. My preferred method of creation was to read a comic story (usually something from the "Little Archie" comic sub-series) and then describe the scene on paper with a ballpoint pen and terrible handwriting. I can't recall why I specifically wrote stories about Little Archie; my best guess is that the little red-headed wiener typically went on adventures that spanned multiple pages, which are more satisfying to narrate than teen

Archie's typical three- or four-page gag comics. (That would be something. "And then Mr. Lodge said, 'Oh boy, here we go again'!")

Unfortunately, this was around the same time my grade 2 teacher got fed up with us idiot children copying information straight out of books for our research projects on robins and whatever. She finally gathered us for a very special Carpet Time, which was a lesson about plagiarism instead of the show-and-tell sessions that Carpet Time was usually reserved for. She also made it clear she'd flay our weaselly little hides if we didn't knock it off.

My little kid brain became a paranoid mess after the discussion because it was incapable of understanding fanworks versus straight-up plagiarism. I stopped writing fanfiction altogether for a while. It's not as if my teacher criticized fanfics specifically. For all I knew, she was a closet Spock/Kirk shipper who had a stack of Star Trek zines stashed somewhere at home. But I stewed in fear of being hauled off to the special wing of jail that existed for seven-year-olds who write fanfiction.

Ultimately, the threat of doing hard time didn't stifle my urge to damage other people's books and movies with my own interpretations. Even as a little child I loved to watch order dissolve into chaos. With a pen in my hand and a licensed character in my head, I could give birth to all sorts of dumb possibilities. I'd been doing my nonsense for some time even before I was introduced to video games, a virgin media that was ripe for effing around with.

The vector for my new sickness was the ColecoVision, a game system my parents brought home after going to a Maple Leafs game. This was 1984, about a year after the North American video game console crash, so they probably snagged the hardware for a song. It's true Atari Inc.'s Ozymandian fall left mass graves of E.T. and Pac-Man cartridges rotting in the desert, but the clearout prices made games and consoles more financially accessible to lower-income families like mine.

Our new ColecoVision was armed with a *Donkey Kong* cartridge, which still ranks in the upper tier of home adaptations for the arcade hit. Eric Bromley, the ColecoVision's designer and engineer, famously fell in love with Donkey Kong while making a business trip to Nintendo's head offices in Japan. Nintendo Life interviewed Bromley about the monkey encounter in September 2010, wherein Bromley admits it only happened because he was looking for the can. (Too much tea.) On his search, he spied one of the original *Donkey Kong* cabinets, and he instantly knew it was a game ColecoVision had to have. A subsequent licensing struggle with Atari spurred Bromley into making the very best *Donkey Kong* console port possible. He even promised Yoko Yamauchi, the daughter of then-Nintendo President Hiroshi Yamauchi, that "Donkey Kong would look like crap on the Atari VCS" (aka the Atari 2600) next to the ColecoVision's port.

Bromley was not bluffing. Donkey is unmistakably gorilla-shaped on the ColecoVision, whereas he resembles an angry mail slot on the Atari VCS. Donkey Kong looked so good on the ColecoVision that I admit I was scared of his mean, pinched white face. He almost never moves in the ColecoVision port; he just stares right through you with pinprick eyes and a deep scowl. I get that data constraints made it impossible for home systems to replicate the goofball animations Donkey Kong performs in his arcade cage, but man, ColecoVision Donkey Kong knew exactly who I pushed on the playground and he was gonna tell my mom.

Once I looked past the scowl, *Donkey Kong* slowly taught me how to play video games. Nintendo's smash arcade hit is an effective tutorial: It tutors you in action basics like running, climbing, jumping, and taking advantage of power-ups when possible. I suppose Nintendo's expertise on teaching people *how* to play games in the first place is one of the reasons it managed to repair the home console market in North America. *Donkey Kong* taught me the ropes (well, vines) of action games, and the varied level design made it worth my while to keep refining my skill. In retrospect, playing my first video game with a ColecoVision controller gave me master class-level training. Moving the ColecoVision's joystick component is like shoving a boulder uphill. I just used the heel of my little kindergarten-diseased palm and did all right for myself.

Donkey Kong's wacky-yet-familiar setting is a good introduction to the bare basics of storytelling in a video game. Donkey Kong absconds with a blonde beauty, Pauline, who is now canonically the mayor of the city wherein the giant ape held her hostage. On paper, *Donkey Kong*'s story doesn't differ much from the thin narrative that drives most arcade games of the era, i.e. "Save innocent people from aliens/giant insects/gorillas." But *Donkey Kong*'s story has one eye-catching twist: Whenever Pauline's would-be rescuer, Mario, reaches the top of a level and gets close enough to touch her, Donkey Kong grimaces, grunts, and snatches Pauline before clambering up to the next level of the game's four-stage loop. A cartoon heart sprite breaks over Mario, and the chase begins again.

These *Donkey Kong* pantomimes aren't exactly cutscenes. Even if they were, they wouldn't be the first; *Pac-Man*, released in arcades a year earlier, features proto-cutscenes between levels where Pac-Man and the ghosts torment each other back and forth. But *Donkey Kong*'s charming interludes put literal faces to its characters. More than that, Nintendo took clever advantage of Universal Studios' 1933 film classic *King Kong*. Thanks to Universal, the image of a giant gorilla climbing a tall structure while hanging onto a girl was already seared into humanity's collective culture. (A fact that got Nintendo into some hot water with Universal's lawyers in 1983, but that's a whole other barrel of monkeys.)

Donkey Kong instantly stood out when it was released in an arcade scene choked with generic space shooters. Its fresh-yet-familiar aesthetic combined with challenging platforming to deliver one of the most influential and important products in Nintendo's hundred-years plus of existence.

The plaster-masked Donkey Kong in the ColecoVision port lacks the silly energy of the arcade Donkey Kong, but a gorilla perched on girders was still an interesting visual in video games at the time. Shortly after my parents brought home our ColecoVision, they bought the Atari 2600 module that slots into the ColecoVision's gaping wound/port — which provided me my first taste of arcade classics like *Asteroids* and *Space Invaders*. Most games developed in the early '80s challenged players to rack up high scores, usually in sci-fi settings littered with simple-looking enemy ships and/or space junk. I don't get a lot of pleasure out of watching numbers go up, so I found myself bored with the Atari 2600 before long.

I still dicked around with video games on rainy days when I couldn't bump around on my friend's BMX bike and rattle my helmet-free brain. *Donkey Kong* on the ColecoVision was usually my go-to on those days. It wants you to chase that high score, but Mario's quest has a real sense of place thanks to its fantastic twists on mundane real world locations like construction sites.

Those pinkish-purple girders, those powder-blue ladders, even Donkey Kong's ghost-white face became the first colours and structures I thought of when someone said "video game." *Donkey Kong* still lacked something I didn't know I was craving from video games at the time, however. Something I couldn't put my finger on. Something neither the Atari 2600 nor the ColecoVision was capable of.

Meanwhile, Nintendo, its hour come 'round at last, crossed the Atlantic and slouched towards Toys "R" Us to be born.

I first saw *Super Mario Bros.* while I was attending a friend's birthday party. I was around seven or eight years old when my relationship with Mario picked up again. I hadn't even thought about the mustachioed working man since putting down *Donkey Kong*, but it was nice to see him again. And he was so *accomplished*! How could I think otherwise when he was the star of *Super Mario Bros.* for the NES, the most influential platforming game of all time? The game that wound up in the living rooms and bedrooms of North American kids everywhere, except for poors like me?

My friend's mother played *Super Mario Bros.* for us as we watched, rapt, surrounded by soft piles of laundry and rumpled blankets. At some point I was expected to detach and attend to my friend in the living room so we could organize a song and dance session about kitty cats.

I wasn't about singing and dancing about kitty cats, though. I was *about* that game my friend's mother was playing in the bedroom, that video game that doubled as a story book. I don't know which useless instinct immediately clued me into the fact *Super Mario Bros.* is an interactive piece of fiction, but in retrospect it was a solid assessment. Based on what I knew at the time, most video games were typically single-screened score-chasers that felt too much like homework. On the Nintendo, a man, a *hero*, strode through a world that accommodated his journey with seamless screen scrolling. His enemies — not squares or squiggles, but identifiable monsters that resembled fungi, florae, animals, and insects — fell before his advance, but could leave behind nasty surprises like ricocheting turtle shells. Mario went under water. He ran across long bridges, dodging killer fish. He explored treetops (or spelunked across cliffs, depending on whom you ask.) He faced off against a dragon-turtle again and again, each encounter more dangerous than the last. And finally, *finally*, the story reaches its conclusion. Mario finally meets the Princess he struggled so hard to save, and — well, I'll just say I remember my mother shouting "Whoa! What a *dog!*" when she first watched us rescue Peach.

Yeah, the very first Princess Peach sprite isn't much to look at by today's standards, but Her Majesty's, er, spartan aesthetics were a necessity at the time. Memory-wise, *Super Mario Bros.* is comparable to a good-sized jpeg. That memory was far better spent on building the journey than building a simple reward like a princess whose face doesn't look like a weird shoe.

And oh, what a journey. Us kids at that birthday party, all sitting agape in those laundry nests like fledgelings, had no way of knowing *Super Mario Bros.* was Nintendo's crowning achievement after years of developing simpler games. We weren't world-savvy, and Japan might have well been Narnia or Oz. From my point of view, Nintendo swooped in out of nowhere and dropped a title that instantly morphed the video games from glorified calculators to a teller of tales.

When you're young, you experience a lot of moments where your mind goes *pop* and you develop a brand-new interest. Experiencing *Super Mario Bros.* for the first time wasn't simply a *pop* moment, though. It was more of a gushing explosion, a foamy mess, a mating of Mentos, Diet Coke, and whatever part of the brain that drives us to sin. Mario took his pudgy little paw in mine and guided me into a new world of stories, stories I didn't merely read but actually became *part* of. Call it rebirth, call it ruination, call it a response to the siren song of capitalism. Whatever you want to call it, video games became as precious to me as my favourite story books.

CHAPTER 2

Suffering for Story

"But thou must!" - *Dragon Warrior*

At some point I smartened up and realized if I wanted to get an NES, I'd have to scrimp for it myself. I scrounged nickels, dimes, and pennies for months at a time. I did extra chores, saved up my allowance, and cashed in on visits to my grandparents (Jewish holidays, more like "CHA-CHING baby!"). I got far enough that my parents took pity on me and promised to fill in the rest if I racked up enough A's in school. Which for me was a task akin to holding ten pounds of steel above my head for a year. (I am not an academic person.) I shook and I swayed as I toiled through grade 6, but I eventually earned enough A's halfway through the year to get my NES. I proceeded to baffle my teacher with micro game reviews when we were asked to journal about our week.

In retrospect, playing NES was good for building up my crummy motor skills. Most parents at the time were too annoyed with NES games to admit their kids got anything out of playing them, but I can't deny my hand-eye coordination became a little tighter because *Super Mario Bros. 3* stapled a raccoon tail to Mario and ordered me to make the fat man fly. I was the kid who needed the weird scissors or rubber pencil doo-hickey that indicated where to put my stupid fingers so I could learn how to spell my own name. The first time I played *Super Mario Bros.*, I lacked the motor skills to jump over World 1-1's first Goomba, but I got the hang of maneuvering Mario's airborne bulk in *Super Mario Bros.* 3 mere months later.

That doesn't mean I actually became *good* at video games — at least not right away. The Super Mario Bros. games are moderate challenges next to the NES' most infamously vein-popping platformers, like 1986's *Castlevania* or 1988's *Ninja Gaiden.* (The latter will try to murder you with so many eagles, it may as well double as a sequel to Alfred Hitchcock's *Birds.*) It's one thing to beat Bowser. It's another thing to successfully hop across platforms that drop, disappear, and otherwise repeatedly betray you like in 1987's *Mega Man.*

My inability to digest NES platformers wasn't entirely my fault. The robust game rental market on this side of the pond did not make Japanese developers very happy. They didn't want kids to hand five bucks to Papa Blockbuster and blast through *Bayou Billy* in a weekend, so they cranked up the stakes. A number of games, including the aforementioned *Ninja Gaiden*, *Castlevania 3*, and *Contra* were purposefully made much harder when they were localized for North America. Levels are more difficult to clear, and checkpoints are further spaced apart.

I rarely banged my head against difficult Atari 2600 games because I got no pleasure out of wiggling a joystick to build up a score, but I was compelled to push through the artificially inflated challenges of even the most frustrating NES games. These games brought something new to the medium: Environment. Dimension. And by extension: stories. As video games' graphics, music, and mechanics became more complex, so too did their narratives. The narrative for *Super Mario Bros.* topped out at "Worryingly energetic Italian man rescues a Princess from a turtle-dragon," but it was the first time I recognized a game's capacity for storytelling. And I was all-in.

I quickly learned the Japanese game studio named Konami usually brought out the best in the NES with its gothic Castlevania games. I also learned Castlevania games are not easily conquered. But that savage challenge wasn't a high enough wall to keep me from Castlevania's stories about tragic curses, rebellious vampire children, and monsters empowered by the night. (This might've been fate; my paternal grandfather was born deep in the Carpathian mountains. I suspect I'm 1/16th werewolf.)

My fascination with Castlevania's gloomy roots drove my determination to finish *Castlevania 3* no matter how difficult it proved to be. The monsters in the localized *Castlevania 3* hit harder, and the wall-clambering pirate monkey-man Grant DaNasty is severely nerfed, which sucks Bluebeard's haunted nuts. Whereas Grant throws daggers by default in the Japanese version of the game (where it was released as *Akumajō Densetsu*, or *Legend of the Devil Castle*,) North American kids have to learn how to fight demons with Grant's pocket knife. This puts the weak little bugger in the midst of every skeleton's death zone, thereby making Grant next to useless. Boo. Boooo!

The final fight against Dracula is still regarded as a nightmare gauntlet in *Akumajō Densetsu*, but in *Castlevania 3*, it's interactive hate mail to North America's rental market and the game-hungry children who kept its gears greased. Dracula has three forms in *Castlevania 3*: First up is a pale guy in a cape wielding a magic wand. He makes fire shoot out of the ground, and if you don't have the reflexes of a chipmunk on amphetamines, main vampire hunter Trevor gets a pillar of fire up his ass. (Don't tell me he's wearing underwear under that doeskin skirt of his. Trevor Belmont is no coward.) Dracula's second form is an amalgamation of tortured faces connected by a giant brain. The fleshy mass floats around the screen, dripping acidic blood that shears off huge chunks of Trevor's health when contact is made. And Dracula's third form is a giant gargoyle that shoots lasers and spawns bottomless pits on the battlefield because eff you.

If you fail to empty all three of Dracula's life bars in *Akumajō Densetsu*, you're sent back to the foot of the iconic moon-washed staircase that has marked the entrance of the Count's innermost quarters since the first Castlevania game. You need only climb those ivy-wrapped stairs to attempt Dracula's first form again. In *Castlevania 3*, you're knocked back to the start of the level. You must run, jump, clamber, and pray through five solid minutes of *Castlevania 3*'s most relentless gauntlet before you're allowed to face (and face, and face) the Count again.

It hurt. It hurt so very badly. But I respected Castlevania's gothic world enough to push through the agony as long as I needed to. I played slowly and thoughtfully. I suffered weeks of failure until I *finally* managed to force the Count to eat one too many boomerangs. I was rewarded with a surprisingly cinematic ending that showed me Trevor standing with Grant on a cliff that overlooked Dracula's castle. Grant let out a cheer as the accursed cathedral suddenly crumbled to dust.

Load-bearing bosses were nothing new in video games even in those early years, but *Castlevania 3*'s ending utilizes custom sprites, cinematic angles, music that's only heard over the ending and credits, and a text crawl that explains how the heroes felt about their victory. I was highly impressed with the effort, even having no idea at the time that Grant's ending is the least impressive of the four that are available. Each of Trevor's companions in *Castlevania 3* gets their own conclusion, with the arguable best ending belonging to Sypha Belnades. Sypha is introduced in the instruction booklet as a male cloaked vampire hunter who favours magic attacks over whacking enemies with "his" staff. When Trevor beats up Dracula with Sypha's help, they stand together on the Cliff of Scrolling Text. Sypha's hood blows backwards and blonde hair cascades over *her* shoulders and she leans into Trevor, who hugs her in return.

I never achieved this ending for myself. *Castlevania 3* awards you one cinematic per runthrough, and the companion you finish it with (if any) determines which ending you see. One playthrough of *Castlevania 3* with Grant was plenty for me, though I'm sad I missed seeing the Sypha ending with my own eyes. I would have absolutely died with glee. The image of the two standing shoulder-to-shoulder in fact resonated so strongly with players that Konami canonically paired the two and made them the most enduring power couple across all Castlevania media.

I came to appreciate how developers like Konami respected games at a level that encouraged them to imitate movies. They leaned into that itch and produced 8-bit cinematics that Atari 2600 games could only have electronic dreams of. *Castlevania 3*'s cinematics hit me hard because of my struggle to earn them, but there are plenty of powerful NES "movie reels" that still remain in my mind's eye: *Ninja Gaiden*'s moonlit duel between two mysterious warriors right there in the game's opening. Mega Man's silent, melancholy walk back home in *Mega Man 2*. The movie-accurate depiction of the Batmobile rushing through Gotham's bruise-purple streets in *Batman*'s opening seconds. Developers didn't have to learn how to make these cinemas, let alone infuse them with life. But they did. And whereas other kids mashed the start button the second they turned the game on, I did not. Dear game-makers, just know that your efforts were acknowledged and appreciated by a ratty little Canadian weirdo whose story-sick mind was subsequently ruined for good.

The problem with accessing all these cinemas is you usually have to finish the game to see that dramatic flourish. I hope I've made it obvious why that was a difficult ask for my young pretzel-fingered self. So when I learned about role-playing games (RPGs), my love affair with video games skyrocketed to an all-out sickness. These hours-long adventures eschewed twitch-based game mechanics for menu commands. They were interactive fairy tales filled with catalogues of mazes and monsters. They were everything I loved about video games, all accessible without having to jump over bottomless pits while dodging pissed-off birds. To put it in the least elegant way possible, I learned early on that RPGs are *exactly my shit.*

No wonder I was one of the six North American children who paid attention when Nintendo tried so, *so* hard to make us fall in love with role-playing games. Console RPGs dominated Japanese charts by 1988 thanks to the monstrously successful *Dragon Quest* series, and Nintendo of America understandably hoped we'd also snatch up these deep, slow journeys into forests and dragon lairs. Nintendo literally pushed free copies of the game into kids' hands after performing an impressive localization that included some redrawn character sprites and objects.

Dragon Quest — renamed *Dragon Warrior* in the west because of a trademark held by the original Dungeons & Dragons publisher TSR — is the reason I contracted terminal RPG wasting disease. Nintendo didn't even have to bribe me to get on board. I wasn't a *Nintendo Power* subscriber, and no subscription meant no free *Dragon Warrior* cart. A friend of my brother's loaned it to us, and once I was hooked, I started to regard the franchise with the same reverence I reserved for Mega Man, Super Mario, and Castlevania.

Unfortunately for Nintendo, I was but one North American RPG convert out of too many disinterested people. The *Dragon Warrior* blitzkrieg didn't endear western gamers to the slower, longer games that were popular with their eastern counterparts.

"That's a very traditional thing for [Japan]. You have to try, try, try, try — and then at the end you can finally get a reward," Dragon Quest creator Yuji Horii told *Gamasutra* in a 2011 interview. "It's like climbing up a steep mountain — you have to keep climbing, climbing, climbing, climbing, and then at the end you finally get to the top of the mountain, and you see the beautiful view."

Japan's early and widespread adoption of computers like the MSX and PC-8800 series probably helped Japanese kids appreciate a slower game like *Dragon Quest.* Most of these computers were incapable of smooth screen scrolling, so developers made text-heavy adventure games and visual novels.

Dragon Quest on the Famicom would feel downright brisk after a diet of still-frame images and pages of text.

North America didn't latch onto the budding home computer market as readily as Europe and Asia, so our selection of computer games was comparably anemic. For most of us, video games resurrected and literally took off running with *Super Mario*, and they kept on running with shooters, action games, and sports games. Even for me, the term "Nintendo game" prompts images of Mario running or the Contra bros shooting. Action verbs. But whereas my mind was wide open to the concept of an interactive storybook, I had a few friends who were horrified at the idea of reading in a game. It's not as if they hated to read, they just couldn't fathom why anyone would want to do it when they could be playing *Bart vs. the World*. But having to read my way through *Dragon Warrior* was my favourite thing about it.

My second favourite thing was that it was easy on my reflexes. I could conquer demanding games like *Castlevania 3* if I poured gallons of effort into the attempt, but I was no platforming wizard. *Dragon Warrior* on the other hand could care less if I had the response time of a tortoise. As long as I put time into grinding my levels, I had direct control over how and when I faced its biggest challenges. I could immerse myself in its medieval setting without fear that a skeleton with a vendetta would knock me off a narrow platform and send me back to the start of the game. Dying in *Dragon Warrior* just costs you half your gold, and while that sucks if you've been bashing Wolf Lords for half an hour to afford a suit of Magic Armour, it's far better than being forced back to zero. *Dragon Warrior* even lets you keep the experience points you scrape up before some asshole Star Wyvern inevitably eviscerates you in the empty, sand-scrubbed streets of Hauksness. It's a drag to hike back to the King every time you want to save your game, but once you do, all your progress is locked up safe and secure. Unless your brother hits "Reset" multiple times against Nintendo's explicit instructions *not* to because it might erase your game data. (It didn't work the one time he tried it, thankfully.)

One roadblock stopped me from sliding completely into the dragon hole: The cartridges for *Dragon Warrior II* and *Dragon Warrior III* were scarce and expensive, especially in Canada. When the original *Dragon Warrior* blowout failed, developer Enix took over the localization and publication of its sequels from Nintendo. Enix did not have the big bucks necessary for a widespread release, so these subsequent Dragon Warriors were not an easy purchase.

My family rented most of our NES games at that point in time. Most video stores preferred to charge five dollars a *day*, and would only rent for a couple of days at a time. RPGs aren't ideal for rushed weekend playthroughs. Even a week was almost never enough to finish an RPG unless I piggybacked off someone else's save file. Luckily, we found an independent shop that loaned out games for a week at a time for five dollars a pop. That was a crazy good deal, and I don't doubt being able to rent RPGs for a week at a time played a key role in nurturing my love affair with the genre.

This wobbly access to NES RPGs unfortunately eroded my affair with the genre. How could I continue loving RPGs if I couldn't play them? I knew *Dragon Warrior IV* was out there somewhere, but I never saw the cartridge in the wild until I started attending retro game expos.

This problem was complicated by the presence of two brothers. I flipped head over heels over the iconic *Dragon Warrior III* after my first week of sampling, and I was prepared to rent it for as many weeks as it took for me to get my fill. But since we had to take turns every week (UGH), I was forced to surrender *Dragon Warrior III* whenever my brothers wanted to rent a hockey game or something horrid involving the Muppets. There was one copy of *Dragon Warrior III* for rent at that store, and more often than not it was in someone else's home when I tried to get it.

If I'd been a sensible kid, I would've strangled my adoration for RPGs right out of my system. I already had to live with the knowledge that Japan got RPGs I could only dream about, games that I'd never see translated if I lived to be a thousand years old. I could never bear to kill that part of myself. (I don't know if it can even *be* killed. It'd probably just spit out the bullet.) Instead, I merely put my RPG love to bed and tiptoed back to action games. I glanced around for new Dragon Warrior games whenever I was at a store or a rental shop, but never caught sight of anything familiar. It was difficult to get quick, accurate news from the Japanese game development scene in the '90s, so I had no way of knowing Enix's American branch had shut down in 1995 because of financial difficulties. I wouldn't see official localizations for Enix's 16-bit Dragon Quest games — including the celebrated *Dragon Quest V* — until years down the road.

Still, *Dragon Warrior III* left a canyon-sized impression on my heart and imagination despite our fleeting time together. We were fated to be separated for years after Roger Rabbit and bad grades killed my NES access. Without games, I was forced to gobble up — and subsequently express — my red-hot love for *Dragon Warrior III* via old-fashioned means like reading and writing.

("I swear Eddie, I didn't kill no Nintendo! Y-y-you gotta believeeve me!")

You know what you did, you gibbering lapine scum. And soon enough, so will everyone.

CHAPTER 3

Can I Borrow this Dragon [Quest] for a Sec?

"I hate doing these stupid projects for school!" - Jay, *Shadow Dragon*

As already stated in this chronicle, I got my own NES in 1991 by saving my pennies and maintaining my good grades. 1991 happened to be the year the Super Nintendo came to North America alongside an ad campaign that made the pack-in game, *Super Mario World*, look like the second coming of Jesus. I didn't know a lot about the Super Nintendo back then, only that it was a grail I couldn't hope to touch in my lifetime.

I was okay with that. Up until that point in my life, I'd only played snippets of the NES's classic games at friends' houses. I'd only seen up to World 3 of *Super Mario Bros. 3*. I'd never gotten anywhere substantial in *Castlevania II: Simon's Quest*. I'd only seen the first few levels of *Cobra Triangle*. Now I could finally delve into these adventures at my own pace and solve their mysteries at my leisure.

Besides, I'd picked up my NES at a perfect time. The coming of the SNES and the rising popularity of the Sega Genesis drove merchants to put deep discounts on games —

especially used games. The NES was still grooving along in its prime as developers learned to use every part of the system. There was no shortage of great games to play. And if I ground my teeth every time some grinning classmate bragged about their Super Nintendo, what of it?

I obviously became a monster for Dragon Quest. Having already played the first and second games, I was primed and ready when *Dragon Quest III,* the RPG that literally every Japanese person fell madly in love with, finally got a localization in March of 1992.

Dragon Quest III was first released in Japan in 1988, and it was by far the deepest, most complex RPG that existed on Nintendo's 8-bit machine until that point. Its depth is still unmatched, save maybe its sequel *Dragon Quest IV* which was released in 1990. (*Dragon Quest IV*'s translation followed closely behind *Dragon Quest III*'s, coming just a few months later in October of 1992. Neither game got a robust release. I would never have even touched *Dragon Quest III* if not for a rental shop that was open-minded enough to carry RPGs.)

Nintendo of America's struggle to make North American kids like RPGs is embedded in legend. It spent a ton of time and effort to localize and distribute the first *Dragon Quest* game, but their efforts were largely a flop. I honestly believe Nintendo would've had far better success had it backed *Dragon Quest III* instead of the first game. The first *Dragon Quest* is revolutionary, but that doesn't mean it's a lot of fun to play. It's a product of 1986; it's slow, it's clunky, and it's tedious to exchange blows with enemies one-on-one. Not even the monster designs by the late great mangaka Akira Toriyama spice up the experience enough to make it worth playing, unless you're nostalgic for getting your ass kicked by a Red Dragon in the depths of the Dragonlord's pitch-black dungeon.

Dragon Quest III had re-arranged Japan's RPG culture by the time Nintendo finally got the first game to North Americans in 1989. Even with the admirable touches Nintendo added to "modernize" Dragon Quest — e.g. hero and NPC sprites that faced in four different directions instead of one — it didn't catch on. 1989 was also the year the NES saw the release of side-scrolling games that are still celebrated by nostalgia-poisoned middle aged folks like myself. Kids ditched the descendent of Erdrick to play *DuckTales*, *Mega Man 2*, and *Ninja Gaiden*, and only a few like-minded weirdos stuck around.

It's wrong to suggest western kids' apathy towards Dragon Quest spilled into the RPG genre, however. Nintendo of America also localized and distributed the original *Final Fantasy*, the RPG masterpiece fronted by SquareSoft game developer Hironobu Sakaguchi. Like *Dragon Quest*, there was a large gap between *Final Fantasy*'s launch on the Famicom (1987) and its launch on the NES (1990). But a year made all the difference on the primal planes of early game development, and *Final Fantasy* was developed specifically to surpass *Dragon Quest*. It still felt kind of archaic in 1990, but its four-player party, side-on battlefield view, in-depth job system (which remains a defining mark of the Final Fantasy series to this day), and surprisingly developed story captured many western imaginations. An October 1994 *EGM* interview with SquareSoft publicity manager Yusuke Hirata reveals *Final Fantasy* sold 700,000 copies on the NES, versus 600,000 on the Famicom. Also consider *Final Fantasy* is a pre-loaded game on the once-coveted NES Classic Mini plug-and-play console. SquareSoft's premiere RPG is parked alongside the NES's heaviest hitters, including *The Legend of*

Zelda, *Castlevania*, the *Super Mario* games, and *Punch-Out!!*. (So to speak.) It's hardly a forgotten classic.

Dragon Quest III is a refinement of *Final Fantasy* in many ways. It uses *Final Fantasy*'s job system, but makes it much easier to experiment with your characters' class changes. You can mix-and-match in ways previously unheard of in console RPGs and create anomalies. Soldiers that use magic! Healers capable of taking a chunk out of monsters! Mass hysteria! Enix built this system on a world-spanning quest that's still considered one of the biggest, heartiest, most well-constructed RPGs of all time. It enraptured Japan to the point that every console generation seemed to spawn at least one remake. In fact, another *Dragon Quest III* remake hit consoles in November 2024, this time in the beautiful retro pop-up "2D-HD" aesthetic made popular by 2018's *Octopath Traveler* for the Switch.

But despite all these revisions and refinements, I can still easily recommend the original Famicom/NES *Dragon Quest III*. It's not my first recommendation; like all 8-bit RPGs, *Dragon Quest III* is a bit of a grind, something the remakes usually alleviate by boosting experience points and gold gains. The point is, any RPG fan of any skill level can play the original release today without having a miserable experience. *Dragon Quest III's* bedrock is unshakeable. If Square Enix somehow finds a way to keep publishing remakes into the coming millenia, I'm confident *Dragon Quest III* will remain as fun in Hell Dimension 6000 (née Earth) as it is now.

While Nintendo threw itself behind promoting *Dragon Warrior*, Enix was unfortunately on its own for *Dragon Warrior III*'s advertising, localization, and distribution. Its reach, needless to say, was significantly diminished without Nintendo's muscle. Maybe there's a reality where Nintendo sent every *Nintendo Power* subscriber a copy of *Dragon Warrior III,* but that hypothetical wasn't reality. Only a small handful of North American Dragon Quest devotees got their hands on *Dragon Warrior III.*

I experienced *Dragon Warrior III* through a series of rentals at our trusty video store. It was prohibitively expensive and elusive in Canada, so going sloppy seconds with some other hero's save file was my only keyhole into Enix's sacred quest. Kudos to the proprietor of the video store who went to the trouble of photocopying *Dragon Warrior III*'s massive 42-page instruction booklet, which is a work of art in itself. It was more of a strategy guide, really, with an illustrated step-by-step walkthrough of the entire journey. Big chain video rental stores rarely included standard instruction booklets with their game rentals, let alone guides. *Dragon Warrior III* is special on its own, but that sheaf of blotched black-and-white paper was my travel brochure for a seemingly boundless fantasy world.

Now presenting a dirty secret: I didn't actually play *Dragon Warrior III* from start to finish until I bought and played the primo Game Boy Colour remake from 2000. Our favoured video store allowed for long rentals, but a week still wasn't near enough time for an RPG novice to clear *Dragon Warrior III.* Plus, as I lamented elsewhere in this tome, having to share game rental weeks with my brothers made subsequent rentals difficult.

Interestingly, my ineloquent patchwork experience with *Dragon Warrior III* might be the catalyst that caused me to fall in love with it. If you rented RPGs in the 90s, you hopefully followed an unspoken rule: The first save file is usually a completed game. Second, third, etc, save files were okay to delete, but don't touch the save file for the "finished" adventure.

My rental copy of *Dragon Warrior III* had one such save file. The party members (all of whom carried sensible names like "John" and "Ted") were at astronomically high levels. They were equipped with the game's best weapons. They were saved just outside the castle of the game's final villain, a reptilian shaman named Zoma. I could walk John and Ted into the creep's lair, pull his pants down, laugh, and step out into a new world full of flowers and sunshine.

I did that more than once, but I also used my borrowed Superfriends to travel all over *Dragon Warrior III*'s vast overworld — and its dark underworld. The Dragon Quest series has a handy-dandy spell called "Zoom" that teleports you to previously-visited landmarks. I made liberal use of Zoom in my travels, but I also hoofed through monster country, bold as brass. I visited towns that thanked me for helping them with demons I never fought myself. I met people who told me about the hero's father, Ortega, who set out on his own quest long ago and is now missing in action. I got to plunge deep into the most dangerous but exciting parts of the game where Toriyama's monster designs become more twisted and dangerous-looking. I'll forever hate the gaping, slobbering grin of Dragon Quest's Troll monsters. Strong as John's party was, I had a hard time standing up to the Trolls' fierce strength. I still had a lot to learn about secondary RPG mechanics like buffs and debuffs.

It's strange to play an RPG "in reverse" like I did with *Dragon Warrior III*, but the experience fertilized my imagination. I only knew how certain side quests turned out, not how they started. I filled in my own blanks, making up small stories as I went from place to place. I also started my own game and raised my own party. I started with the Hero, a Soldier, a

Pilgrim (Cleric), and a Wizard. I don't recall any names I used, but I doubt they were tasteful. I didn't come anywhere close to catching up with the Legend of John, but I still experienced a good chunk of *Dragon Quest III*'s early game. It made me feel like I'd truly immersed myself in a story head-to-toe, and it just so happens that's a *great* feeling if you're me.

Sadly, a bucket of ice water was soon thrown onto our soul-melding love. *Dragon Warrior III* was a rental game; it had to go back to the store within a week. I even faced a test of honour by returning the game to the video store's drop-box, since the store itself was closed down for renovations. Truthfully if my mom hadn't been there, I 100% would have ripped the game off, battered photocopied instruction booklet and all.

My dreams of a reunion with *Dragon Warrior III* took an additional blow when my NES decided it was time to sail west across the sea. It's a well-known piece of bar trivia that the NES' VCR-style shell was a clever cuckoo's egg designed to fool parents into thinking they were buying an "Entertainment System," not another video game console destined to die alongside the Atari VCS. It was a brilliant bit of commercial subterfuge, but it also battered the shit out of our games' connectors and gave us those blinking orange-and-grey TV screens that still flash in every Gen X kids' nightmares. Sometimes blowing inside the cartridge (ooooh yesss) helped get games working again. Sometimes we were just SOL.

My NES stopped working reliably around the same time a kid down the street loaned us *Who Framed Roger Rabbit?*, an action-adventure game designed by Rare in 1989. Rare is a good studio but *Who Framed Roger Rabbit?* is not a good game, which is why it's still popular fodder for the furnace that feeds the "What the Hell is This Crap?" sector of YouTube. It's opaque, it's slow, and it's devoid of the movie's fun and joy. In fact, *Who Framed Roger Rabbit?* for the NES is just plain eerie. Every character's face is blank, which is a weird stylistic choice in a world where Toons are supposed to make exaggeratedly wacky expressions. Honestly, I can't think of a more appropriate vector for the STD that rendered my NES near-unplayable. I might not be able to prove Roger Rabbit polluted my console's innards with his filth, but I know the truth. God is with me.

God was not with me when I entered grade 7 as the class of '92. For reasons I never discovered, I was put in the "second" class. That is, the class with the kids who, er, didn't get the best marks or needed extra help with their work. Or needed to be coached off the ceiling every morning. Admittedly, I was a good writer and I read ahead of my grade level, but my grammar and spelling were atrocious. My wobbly penmanship was moreover befitting of a grade 3 kid who'd been slammed in the back of the head with a red VKM kickball, not a grade 7 student. I struggled with math, and by "struggled," I mean "couldn't get the hang of subtraction." Maybe putting me in the problem kids' class (let's just call it what it was) seemed like the right choice at the time.

It wasn't. Something strange happened in that class, something that had never happened before and never happened again after that: I got bored, and I acted out accordingly. The worksheets I was being handed were insultingly easy, not even worth doing. This is supposedly a telltale sign of a "gifted" student, but the idea never entered my mind because I was long past being funneled off into that exclusive academic club. I was tested as a gifted child in elementary school, but I did not pass. I recall the test involved some triangles and squares that baffled me like pagan symbols. I poked at answers until someone took my worksheet from me with slow pity.

If the criteria for being gifted had involved writing an on-the-spot story about a rabid unicorn that dripped cotton-candy foam from its diseased chops as it hunted for elves to eat, I would've leg-dropped that test. But the '90s public school system could only dedicate so much extra time and instruction to a weird kid who had no stinking idea how some triangles and squares were supposed to relate to each other. Long story short, I did not do any of my assigned work for the first half of grade 7. My first report card arrived, and my marks s*uuuuuucked.*

Bad marks meant no Nintendo in our house. It was an iron rule, enforced until the next report card showed significant improvement. So I was without my NES for much of 1992, which didn't hurt me as badly as you might think because the goddamn EZ Bake Oven-looking piece of crap barely worked after Roger Rabbit gave it syphilis. It was time for me to grasp the grail that I hardly let myself look upon two years ago: The Super Nintendo. The SNES. The 16-bit miracle machine that may as well have been the Popemobile for how far out of my reach it was. But I was a thrifty, patient child, and I sometimes even remembered to stash my money box somewhere my younger brother couldn't raid it for cigarette change. (I also extorted money from my family by taking the Passover afikomen for ransom at least once. Nobody ever thinks to look in the toilet tank.)

I still would have made a deal with Beelzebub to fix my NES if I could play *Dragon Warrior III* on it one more time, but that was never going to happen. I knew I had a better chance of meeting the Lord of Darkness than I did of ever touching

Dragon Warrior III ever again. For a generation raised in an era where epic-length games are a download away it might seem silly to think of a game as "gone forever." (Even as developers yoink games off their digital marketplaces and hope nobody notices.) Games weren't always an easy acquisition in the good ol' days, though. Fetching a game at Toys "R" Us meant looking at a wall of game boxes before taking a tag up to a person in a booth surrounded by plastic walls. That exchange alone made buying video games feel solemn and sophisticated. NES emulators were unheard of in 1992, let alone the online infrastructure to distribute them. *Dragon Warrior III* only existed as a cartridge, and no cartridge meant no *Dragon Warrior III*.

No NES also meant no video games that summer. *Dragon Warrior III*'s absence left me with an appetite for fantasy stories, so I spent a lot of time in the library near our house. It was small compared to the multi-storied libraries located elsewhere in the city, but it had the Dragonlance books by authors Margaret Weis and Tracy Hickman. The first trilogy, the Dragonlance Chronicles, contains *Dragons of Autumn Twilight*, *Dragons of Winter Night*, and *Dragons of Spring Dawning*, all published across 1984 through 1985. I immediately flung myself into that nonsense and had a ball even though I knew little about TSR's Dungeons & Dragons table-top RPG phenomenon. Everything I knew about D&D was owed to the Marvel Productions cartoon, which I didn't watch very often.

[Random trivia drop, my parents have a picture of me and my brothers in Halloween '80-something, and my younger brother's "costume" is just a plastic smock stamped with the leering, trollish grin of the D&D cartoon's squat "Dungeon Master" character. I remember there was a mask to go along with the smock — which featured Dungeon Master's leering, trollish grin, go fig — but it was busted long ago. I wasn't much older before cops and teachers started begging parents not to buy these dark, worryingly flammable apron-mask combos that were clearly designed by someone who *wanted* to blind children with shitty masks and shepherd them into traffic. That would be a great plot for another divergent Halloween movie in the vein of "Season of the Witch," but I digress…]

The "video game RPGs to Dragonlance" pipeline was a wide one, as I'd learn when I met others like me online. The Dragonlance books, especially the first three, have a distinct game-like feel to them. Console RPGs like *Dragon Quest* and D&D are first cousins. I had already massaged my brain into accepting the unique, halting way video games tell their stories, so I had no problem following the same style of narrative in novels. Every challenge the party faces in "Dragons of Autumn Twilight" is laid out like a D&D module that progresses in your head as you read along. The party gathers in an inn under troubled circumstances. A ruckus forces them on the road, and they're quickly shepherded into their destiny — which is nothing less than "Push back the encroaching influence of the Goddess of Evil, Takhisis." ("Takhisis" being the Dragonlance universe's name for Tiamat, the five-headed dragon queen who rules over the darkness in many D&D settings.) But before the party can even dream of taking on Takhisis and restoring balance to Krynn, they have to level up with modules. They have to get into skirmishes. They have to enter caves to find ancient, powerful weapons. They have to disarm traps in enemy-infested ruins and dungeons.

In one incident, the team is badly surprised by the arrival of an enemy none of them have ever seen before: A group of low-ranking bipedal lizard-men that are eventually revealed to be "Draconians." Draconians are essentially bio-manufactured pests that are an ideal fight for a group of adventurers. They even transform into stone for a few moments after they're killed, entrapping the weapon of the person who slayed them. Oh no! -1 for slash/stab attacks! But the party works around it, as a healthy party does. Then they find a tunnel that contains an ancient sword that once belonged to an elf king. Oh no! The party's leader, Tanis, is a half-elf, so the close walls of the tunnel chafe his elven blood something fierce. He suffers a major debuff during a boss fight with a giant slug! But everything is OK after the party rallies and everyone plays their literal roles with growing confidence. And they get a weapon that ultimately helps them against one of the story's final bosses: A red dragon.

I didn't know it at the time, but Dragonlance even played a direct role in the creation of two characters from *Phantasy Star,* the classic 1987 Sega Master System RPG created by the late and much-missed Rieko Kodama. Noah, *Phantasy Star*'s mysterious and ageless blue-haired wizard, is based on Raistlin, Dragonlance's own frail magic user and perpetually suffering pretty boy. Odin, *Phantasy Star*'s triple-muscled meathead who hits stuff, is based on *Dragonlance*'s Caramon, Raistlin's twin brother and empty-headed watchdog.

It's a compelling character dynamic. Kodama talked about the contrast in an interview with Sweden's *LEVEL* game magazine, which was translated by Swedish game journalist Tobias Bjarneby and published in 2022 on TimeExtension.com. Kodama admitted to *LEVEL* that she turned down Raistlin's "Asshole" dial a little bit when she created Noah. "Noah is far more gentle and a better person than Raistlin, but may be similar in the fact that they are both low in physical strength despite their powerful magic," she said.

I will also gladly eat my hat if Vanillaware artist and character designer George Kamitani didn't cast an eye at Raistlin when he designed the Wizard character for the 2013 fantasy belt-scrolling beat-em-up *Dragon's Crown.* No surprise Kamitani made his iteration of Raistlin look sexy as hell. That man can put curves on a triangle.

It was natural for me to want to write my own epic fantasy "novel" now that I'd gorged myself on dragon meat. I put pen to paper (or dull pencil to crappy school-grade newsprint) and started my first serious writing project. I made my own characters instead of borrowing someone else's characters from a game. I made my own world, with its own geography, florae, and faunae. I made my own heroes, even though they were dipwads, and I made my own villain, even if he was just the Dragonlord in a cool jacket. Dragonlance and *Dragon Warrior III* had put me in the mood to explore boundless fantasy worlds, and I used that inspiration to make something that was unique to me.

I didn't come close to finishing that novel, even though I did have an outline for it. An actual whole-ass plan for the story with a real ending and everything. Just imagine. Talk about the one superpower I want back from my childhood.

I still have the pile of paper that passes for the start of my first novel. My handwriting never improved, so the penciled text resembles the jagged, feathery tendrils that jut from the head of The Boiled One. (Don't look him up, he's scary.) There is a clump of staples in the corner of the story because I had to add chapters to the tome one by one. Not every staple in the corner is necessary — one of my friends just grabbed the story from me and decided to slam it with the stapler over and over. Again, bad kids' class.

Bad kids' class or not, over-stapled mess or not, writing that story made me realize how fun and easy it was to put my imagination to work. I wouldn't have taken that step if *Dragon Warrior III* hadn't taken me on an interactive adventure with its perfectly-measured story text, unforgettable monster designs, near-perfect music score, and struggles against dangerous foes. I still can't get through it without concocting some kind of story for my otherwise-blank party dudes, and *Dragon Warrior III*'s myriad setpieces make that an easy task. I've always been a narrator at heart, and the best experiences are the ones that are easy to narrate.

And narrator still I am, here and now. Or a copywriter for commercial blogs and website hubs. Whatever brings in the dosh. (Usually the corporate stuff, unfortunately.) Maybe I should have moved further into that space and earned an actual grown-up salary instead of fighting dumpster rats for pizza crusts. But then I wouldn't have been able to visit Japan in 2018 to preview *Dragon Quest XI*. I wouldn't have been able to meet series creator Yuji Horii and tell him how *Dragon Quest III* deeply inspired me as a writer, a rando white chick from the Canadian tundra who only got to experience it because the stars aligned.

I heard some time later that Horii was touched to hear all that. Which is a humbling but life-affirming realization that I'll gladly carry through the rest of my life, and into my grave. Along with whatever eviction notices I'll pile up in my sunset years. And the over-stapled novel I called…

[*Pause, sigh*]

Shadow Dragon.

That's pretty much the title you'd expect from a young author who was nursed on video games and weaned on Dragonlance novels. Looking back at the work is about as fun as looking at my vomit, but to be fair both things can give you a good idea of what's going on inside of you. Shadow Dragon is inelegant, but I'm also impressed at how I got ahead of some now-popular fantasy tropes. The story is about two young boys named Jay and Kevin who spill hot chocolate on their report about medieval knights and that kind of crap, so they run to the library to do more research. The two find an appropriate book (after searching on the "computer" for a suitable tome; card catalogues were endangered even by the early '90s), and are then sucked into the medieval world in said book. So, hey! *Shadow Dragon* was a proto-isekai.

"Isekai" refers to a sub-genre of fiction, especially manga and anime, that features protagonists who are resurrected in different, often fantastical worlds after dying in our world. These deaths tend to be violent, e.g. the protags will often get demolished by a kei truck. Apparently Japanese farmers drive to kill.

Truthfully, I probably based the premise of *Shadow Dragon* on "The Neverending Story" or C.S. Lewis' Narnia books or any other book series I read about kids getting magically pulled into fantasy worlds. These rides to Imagination Land were usually non-fatal — barring "The Last Battle," I guess. Now *there's* an isekai. But no, Jay and Kevin are alive when they are pulled into the book's fantasy kingdom (which I forgot to name beyond "The Kingdom"). That doesn't mean their new kingdom home cares if they live or die, and the boys are signed up for a tournament by page three. The first knight they come across conscripts them for missions that include jousting, assassination, and baby-dragon catching for no better reason than "You dudes look weird. I bet you bleed real good."

The school year ended before I wrote my planned epic ending for *Shadow Dragon.* I don't think I even came close, because writing the story taught me something about myself: I can plot, I can outline, I can chart a course for my characters, and I can guesstimate how many words or chapters I might wind up writing, and it won't matter a smidge. Whatever monster governs my thought process is guaranteed to look at something off the path and gasp "Ohh, what's that?" as it grabs the wheel and steers both of us into madness.

It took me three pages to send these two kids from the library to the dungeons of some random kingdom, but by the end of the school year the plot started diverting to subplots that developed characters in surprising ways. Jay and Kevin found friends in the kingdom: An orphaned boy named Timmy (not a name I would choose in a post-*South Park* world) and a mysterious man named Eric. When the tournament starts, Jay straight-up murders the opposing knight in a pretty badass "kill or be killed" moment that would probably earn a phone call home in this day and age. Jay and Kevin are soon informed the tournament is actually a front to train up a champion who can take on the "Dragon King" from the neighbouring kingdom, whose armies of dragons are tearing up the good kingdom's wyvern-based defenses. (I worked hard on the "Dragon King" name. Actually, no. I didn't.) With no obvious way home and nothing else to do, Jay and Kevin agree to stay and unseat the monarch. Circumstances eventually lead to Eric revealing he's the son of the Dragon King, but he became estranged with his father after being emotionally manipulated into doing his bidding. Eric is pretty OK with the idea of his evil father getting merc'd, so he joins up with the boys' cause.

It's telling that Jay and Kevin's first task in *Shadow Dragon* takes up a few pages while the second trial plus miscellaneous plot drama takes up the rest of the "book." Kevin takes point on the second trial, which involves capturing a baby shadow dragon. I wrote these titular beasts to be small but incredibly vicious and highly venomous. They also made their nests in tall trees, which makes for a pretty action-packed trial — especially when Kevin is cornered by an adult shadow dragon while kidnapping its hatchling. The party rides to safety, but not before the baby dragon bites Kevin and sends him into a half-dead limbo state. Kevin, now trapped in the Underworld, must find his way back to his body before he succumbs entirely to the poison, or until he pisses off the Warden of the Underworld badly enough to earn a one-way ticket to actual Hell.

Oh, and also Jay and Kevin are descendents of a long-dead hero named the Black Duke. Kevin meets the Black Duke in purgatory and discovers he's a sour, washed-up fraud. My plan was to have the Duke see the light and sacrifice his soul to help Kevin escape back to the world of the living, but alas I never completed that redemption arc.

Shadow Dragon is a 50-car pile-up. It's my young self screaming and throwing bits and pieces of my mind and heart at pulpy grey newsprint. Its references to Dragon Quest are a bit blatant, between Jay and Kevin being the descendents of the Black Duke (not that I ever figured out how the fantasy world connects to our world) and the Warden of the Underworld being a multi-headed serpent named Orochi. The latter point is funny because I technically didn't rip *anyone* off: The Orochi is a snakelike monster from Japanese myth, and *Dragon Quest III* simply borrows the beast for a subplot. For years I thought I'd lifted Orochi wholesale from the game.

Shadow Dragon also has less-obvious influences from things I remember liking at the time. There are plot niblets from Dragonlance, Stephen King's underrated fantasy novel *Eyes of the Dragon*, Choose Your Own Adventure books — and, unsurprisingly, video game-based cartoons like *Captain N: The Game Master* and especially *The Legend of Zelda*. There's an episode of *Zelda* wherein Link is indeed killed, but it's the '90s so he's not allowed to be totally dead. Ghost Link and flesh Zelda travel to Ganon's lair to retrieve Link's body, and Zelda lets slip that maybe she loves Link "a little," which is why she can see him. It's one of the better episodes of the show, and I guess it made an impact when I first saw it. Adventure? Mushy stuff? Dead bodies? Sign me up.

But there's more going on in the story than warmed-over tropes from the media I was into at the time. The aforementioned shadow dragons building nests in trees is a little different; dragons typically have lairs in mountains or forest caves. A teacher once pointed out the myriad squirrels' nests formed high up in the city's trees, and it fascinated me to learn birds weren't the only animals that built nests. If squirrels, why not dragons? I also like the idea of smaller dragons making up for their lack of physical presence with attitude and venom. I've always been fond of small, dangerous things.

There's a quick mention of the kingdom using wyverns to defend itself against the Dragon King's trained dragons, and this is interesting. Even as a child I knew the difference between a wyvern (a dragon with two legs) versus a dragon (which is a dragon). I had a neat idea going on with this war where "underdeveloped" drakes wouldn't stand a chance versus the beefy four-legged boys. Pop culture has since merged dragons and wyverns; House Targaryen's scaly bioweapons only have two legs and they're capable of wreaking immeasurable havoc. Nevertheless, I carried the old lore when I was a child, and I carry it now. Dragons and wyverns are separate "animals."

(An aside: What few drawings I made for the story contain my interpretation of a wyvern, which is more eagle-like than anything. Again, Dragon Quest takes the blame. The earliest localizations for *Dragon Warrior* translated the "Chimaera" monster as "Wyvern." The monster in question actually has *no* legs and looks like a cross between a snake and a vulture. In other words, Dragon Quest's wyverns/chimaeras look nothing like the traditional depictions of either mythological beast. The wyverns in my story were more reptilian than their direct inspiration, but I did adopt one Toriyama-ism: My wyverns had feathered wings versus dragons' batlike wings. It's a good example of me adding a twist to a traditional heraldic creature — which Toriyama had altered to begin with!)

I also find it interesting that the nameless kingdom seems like a grounded place despite me describing occasional fantastic happenings like dragons living in trees. Jay and Kevin aren't assigned character classes or jobs, a very popular trope in modern fantasy works thanks to Dungeons & Dragons' monster popularity surge. They're lamers when they fall into Book Land, and they'd only started learning how to handle normal maces and swords by the time I stopped writing. I at least remember having plans for Kevin to tame the baby dragon as a pet because why the hell wouldn't he? That's badass.

In fact, *Shadow Dragon* is badass. It has jokes and moments of brevity, but it has an earnest honesty that demonstrates I was serious about the project. I treated a lot of my major writing projects, even the Mega Man fanfictions that were a mere few years from being born, as glorified shitposts. If I kept people laughing at my jokes, they were less likely to turn on me and my writing. But nothing about *Shadow Dragon* is a shitpost. I saw a new world in *Dragon Warrior III* and yearned to mirror it, but what emerged from the loins of my brain (ugh, sorry) was a new animal altogether that I was compelled to nurture. I can't say a video game was the entire reason I built a new world with its own flora and fauna, but I acknowledge *Dragon Warrior III* was a valid catalyst — the same as *Minecraft* or other games might be valid catalysts for kids' creative works today. That's why I will never blow raspberries at the worlds and characters kids invent, even if they're clearly *Genshin Impact* with the serial numbers filed off. No matter how messy and cringe-inducing the final product winds up being, what matters is that the pen touched the page.

CHAPTER 4

"You're Not Owed a Happy Ending" and Other Writing Lessons from a Big Tree

"You are hereby banished from Potos village. Now, get out of here!"
- villager, *Secret of Mana*

In 1994, my hibernating thirst for RPGs grunted and started to shake itself awake. This turned out to be good timing. Being a Super Mario freak, I chose to defend "uncool" Nintendo over the "hip" and "with it" Sega during the '90s console wars, and fighting with my playground peers over billion dollar corporations was starting to turn my brain into swiss cheese. Getting reacquainted with RPGs proved to be a much better use of my time.

The Sega Genesis had (and still has!) some great RPGs, but the genre took root and germinated on the SNES like a hothouse. Getting back into RPGs made me realize only the SNES could give me *Secret of Mana*, *Final Fantasy VI*, *Breath of Fire II*, and *Chrono Trigger*. In time, I realized I had chosen… wisely. My mind and heart returned from the frontlines and healed.

"In time." It took me a little while to realize RPGs didn't start and end with the Dragon Warrior series that I assumed was dead. My brother spent part of the '90s running a BBS (kids, ask your parents) from a Commodore 64 we'd inherited from a friend of my dad for some reason, and I used that BBS just long enough to learn about Squaresoft from another user. "Try *Secret of Mana*," they said.

In retrospect, *Secret of Mana* is a great name for a video game. You hear a title like that and you think, "What *is* the secret? Is it ever revealed?" That inherent mystery might be why Japan has since adopted the "Mana" title to use with, or instead of, the series' original name – "Seiken Dentetsu," or "Legend of the Holy Sword." It's an interesting example of '90s Nintendo's strict policies against religious terms and imagery uplifting a game instead of stunting it. "Holy" was verboten by these rules, but the localized title is more intriguing.

I was already a fan of The Legend of Zelda, especially the dangerous, sprawling world you get to explore in 1987's *Zelda II: The Adventure of Link* for the NES. *Secret of Mana* is likewise an action RPG, a sub-genre that tends to be more user-friendly than traditional RPG menu-based combat. *Secret of Mana*'s sword-swinging combat already felt familiar thanks to the time I spent with *Zelda II: The Adventure of Link*. Interestingly, *Zelda II* is also one of very few Legend of Zelda games where Link explicitly levels up his stats to become stronger — the mark of a true RPG, and something most Legend of Zelda games lack. *Zelda II: The Adventure of Link* is a strange animal, but its emphasis on collecting experience points to get stronger helped me realize how RPG mechanics need not be restricted to menus and turn-based battles.

I fell in love with *Secret of Mana* in about two seconds with the help of its bewitchingly lush title screen. The logo for *Secret of Mana*'s developer, Squaresoft (a name I'd soon hold as close to my heart as a spouse) is accompanied by a few wafting notes of whale song, a naturally haunting sound that's made even more mysterious-sounding by the SNES' audio compression algorithms. *Secret of Mana*'s composer Hiroki Kikuta once explained in a 2014 Reddit AMA that he wanted players to associate the size and majesty of whales with the Mana Tree, the great tree that's central to Secret of Mana's story. Just as whales loom over every other member of the animal kingdom, the Mana Tree towers over all the life it governs in the world.

It's hard to forget *Secret of Mana*'s lush green intro with its scrolling text perfectly synced to Kikua's "Angel's Fear," a staggeringly wonderful piece of video game music that builds up from a handful of hesitant piano notes to a sweeping synthetic orchestra. Looking at that primo attract mode now, I recognize it's another example of *Secret of Mana*'s preference for letting nature and the environment explain things to the player. I go ga-ga for nature metaphors and can't keep my grubby hands off them. I cast animals as heralds, let the trees exchange gossip. And now I suspect *Secret of Mana* taught me a few things about humankind's relationship with nature, another topic I cannot walk away from. We've barely cleared Squaresoft's logo and we've already experienced thoughtful and subtle exposition about *Secret of Mana*'s world.

And *Secret of Mana* was the first RPG I played that offered me a real taste of the stories the genre is capable of telling. *Dragon Quest* through *Dragon Quest III* have stories, but they're not especially character-driven. True to *Wizardry* and the other dungeon crawling western epics that Yuji Horii paid tribute to with Dragon Quest, *you* are the hero. You might have a background as the prince of a monster-threatened kingdom (*Dragon Quest II*) or you might be the child of a mighty hero who is doomed/fated to follow in their father's footsteps (*Dragon Quest III*), but *Secret of Mana* was my first experience with an RPG that took the story out of my hands and gave it to a spiky-haired orphan who plunges down a waterfall while playing with his friends. He's unharmed by the descent, but he does an oopsie when he pulls a sacred sword out of its protective resting spot and brings a plague of monsters down upon the village that raised him. He's thrust into a journey to save the world with nothing but the clothes on his back, a rusty sword, and a pocketful of candy he earned by murdering legless rabbits with said sword on the way back to the village. Epic. Eat it, Shakespeare.

The hero, whose default name in Japan is "Randi" (an admittedly weird moniker for a hero; it makes me think of a tomcat catching scent of an upwind female), is expelled from his town when its Elder espies the boy's sword. He reveals the faint magic in the sword Randi pulled from its stone was all that stood between the villagers and a plague of monsters. The Elder's anger is vindicated when a giant Mantis Ant burrows underneath the middle of the town and pulls the village idiot into the abyss with it. Randi drives the monster back, but his efforts just reward him with a one-way ticket out of his home town. Worse, he's stuck with some dumb rusty sword that he never asked for, and nobody will take off his hands because "It's cursed" / "It's your destiny to wield it."

And the villagers aren't joking when they tell him not to come back. They even station a man who looks like a blonde Ned Flanders at the entrance to Randi's home village, Potos. His only job through the entire game is to tell Randi to get lost if he tries to come back home. It's funny, and also a little demoralizing. Imagine if you have a falling-out with your parents and they not only kick you out of the house, they also pay a guy to stand at the door so he can tell you to sling your hook when you try to return.

Randi's sad expulsion from his home is a memorable way to start an adventure. RPG heroes lose their homes all the time, but usually through an attack by enemy forces, or else through some freak act of nature that's supposed to demonstrate that all is not well in the game's world. It's rarely because of a mistake of the hero's own doing. *Secret of Mana*'s general narrative is storybook simple, but it subverts RPG story tropes in ways that still surprise me when I think back on them.

One side character is a fiery-tempered girl of noble birth named Primm (sometimes spelled as "Purim," which is also the name of a Jewish holiday wherein participants are encouraged, nay, *expected* to get crunk on Manischewitz) who's trying to catch up with her lover who was sent on a dangerous mission. There's also Popoi, a sprite child who was washed into the underground kingdom of dwarves after a storm hit their village. Popoi says they want to get back home, but they actually just want to hang around and start shit because they're a swindler and a trickster. A lot goes wrong for *Secret of Mana*'s young heroes while they chase their individual goals while also attempting to save the world. And the three of them are key figures in the most important writing lesson *Secret of Mana* taught me: Video games don't owe you a happy ending. Same as books, same as movies.

Mana series developer and designer Koichi Ishii planned for *Secret of Mana* to be a dark and grim game as far back as its conception, when it was a clump of ideas for the ill-fated SNES CD add-on. Nintendo canceled the add-on in 1991, which forced Squaresoft to retreat and continue developing

Secret of Mana for the much smaller SNES cartridge format. That included cutting out parts of the story, Ishii admitted. "[T]he original version of *Secret of Mana* was not at all the same game as we eventually released," he said in a 2006 interview with the Swedish magazine *LEVEL*.

Secret of Mana was always intended to be a game for children, so it rocks that Ishii aimed to traumatize us from day one. I suppose *Secret of Mana* doubled as my introduction to the nature of Japanese fairy tales, which are more on the grim (and Grimm) side than western fables. Christopher Kincaid, author of "Come and Sleep: The Folklore of the Japanese Fox," explores the lack of sunny conclusions on his blog, Japan Powered.

"If you read Japanese folklore, you notice how different the endings seem against Western stories," he wrote in a 2021 article titled Unhappily Ever After: the Endings of Japanese Fairy Tales. "In most Japanese folktales, people die in the end. Happily-ever-after endings stand out because of their rarity."

Deaths do indeed occur in *Secret of Mana,* but thanks to Nintendo of America's oft-bananas censorship policies at the time, the English script was forced to soften these events. People "got caught" by the enemy, or they "fell," or they "faded away." The wordplay admittedly blunts the sting of some of *Secret of Mana*'s harder moments. It also makes an already-troubled English script more opaque than it needs to be. It's one thing to cut bad words from a game, but Nintendo of America's enduring death denial irritated me as a kid. We all die. Why is that a controversial theme to explore in a video game?

It's no surprise tragedy drives *Secret of Mana*'s sad final act. Again, Ishii always intended to show us the darker side of

Japan's fairy tales, and the respect he has for video games as a storytelling medium is obvious from the get-go. Primm's story, for example, engaged me from the start. It was rare for women to have decent representation in '90s video games, and Primm is a gem. Here is a woman trained in martial arts who plunges into a haunted forest to save her boyfriend and subsequently kicks a bunch of wolfmen in the nards.

Primm is thankfully not one of the vapid "girlboss" characters that rose up from the proto-muck of corporations' earliest attempts at inclusivity. Her story feels genuine. Primm is nobility, so her father sets her up for an arranged marriage with some blueblood while also conspiring to send her boyfriend Dyluck on a suicide mission to slay a witch. Not only does Primm tell her dad to bugger off (going as far as to say she hates him, which made me gasp a little as a kid. It's a powerful word to use on a parent!), she strikes out on her own to find her lover.

Dad's job for Dyluck *does* turn out to be a suicide mission — a slow one. Dyluck confronts the forest witch who zaps him to parts unknown as soon as Primm catches up to him. This pattern is repeated throughout the game: Sightings of Dyluck are used as bait to lure the young warriors into dangerous territory, and then the captive Dyluck is yanked away whenever Primm is within touching distance. The closest thing the couple have to a reunion is when *Secret of Mana*'s antagonist, the undead wizard Thanatos, controls Dyluck to fool Primm into getting close enough to steal her life force.

When Randi, Primm, and Popoi face off against Thanatos in the last room of the game's final dungeon, the Mana Fortress, he finally explains that Dyluck's soul harbors a sealed-away dark power that makes him an excellent candidate to be a brand new Thanatosmobile, a.k.a. a new flesh vessel. But the spiritual transfusion fails when Dyluck uses his powers to freeze Thanatos in place just long enough to say goodbye to Primm and implore Randi to take care of her before he kills himself to prevent the wizard from inheriting a young new body. Oofah.

Meanwhile, Randi's singular mission in *Secret of Mana* is to reach the fabled Mana Tree and ask it to restore full power to the Mana Sword he pulled from its rock cradle back in Potos. It's an arduous task that involves traveling to eight Mana Seed sanctuaries scattered across the world. Randi slashes his way through forests filled with psychotic pink rabbits (again, the legless kind), climbs mountains, rescues a baby dragon, labors through the ruins of a subway station — more on that jolly locale later on — and is shot out of a cannon *several* times before he's finally allowed to enter the Pure Land, the sacred grove containing the Mana Tree.

Unfortunately, Randi isn't quick enough. Thanatos manages to use the planet's dwindling supply of life energy, Mana, to resurrect the Mana Fortress, an ancient floating weapon. As soon as Randi claps his eyes on the Mana Tree and tells his friends how happy he is to have finally made it, Thanatos rolls over to the Pure Land and metaphorically spin-kicks the Mana Tree with his new toy. It topples, and Randi awakens in front of a burned-up stump. It's all that remains of the Tree that governed all life just moments ago.

The Tree is Randi's long-missing mother, by the way. It's not made clear in *Secret of Mana*'s initial translation, but after giving birth to Randi and dropping him off at Potos, she slunk away to grow into a Mana Tree and become the protector of the world. It's a Mana Tribe thing, apparently. Thanatos' attack leaves the Tree with just enough power to unlock the Mana Sword's true potential, with time left over to say goodbye to the son she never had a chance to raise. Yaaaaay!

Popoi gets a two-for-one misery special. First, they do indeed find their way back home to the village of the Sprites, only to discover the Empire has sacked it and killed most of its inhabitants. Then, in the game's very last moments, they recall something their grandfather said: Sprites are creatures of Mana. If Mana disappears from the world, so will Popoi. Popoi unloads all this on Randi at the moment he's forced to make a stand against *Secret of Mana*'s final boss, the Mana Beast. The Beast is simply a force of nature that aims to restore the world's depleted Mana stores, but doing so means ending all human life and starting anew. If the Mana Beast is killed, people will survive, but all Mana will truly vanish from the world — along with Popoi. The answer is unfortunate but clear, and Popoi insists that Randi slays the Mana Beast. The determined little Sprite fights alongside his friends one last time, then vanishes the moment the Beast is destroyed. *Secret of Mana*'s post-credits scene shows us Popoi one last time as a shimmering, ghostly figure in the Sprite village. The game freezes on a final screen of Popoi looking up at the moon, alone, as the night wind plays through their hair. Popoi is not dead, per se — which indicates some tendrils of Mana survived the Apocalypse — but somehow it's worse knowing they're still "alive," but in a state where they'll never be able to see their friends again.

Hip, hip, *hooray*! What fun!

At its core, *Secret of Mana* is a game about the importance of balance, preservation, and living in harmony with nature.

"Save nature" was an extremely common basis for children's media in the '90s. On the television, Captain Planet — a green-haired superhero with a perpetual case of cyanosis — battled sneering bad guys who dumped toxic waste into rivers for the helluvit. The poofy-haired Suntots beat up the mean, dirty Smoggies. (Don't feel bad if you have no idea who the Suntots or Smoggies are, they're products of Canada and France, and when Canada and France work together, chaos is born. Hence the Donkey Kong Country cartoon.) Sonic the Hedgehog famously battled Dr. Robotnik's encroaching wave of pollution in the Sonic the Hedgehog Saturday morning cartoon, a.k.a. "SatAM." The cartoon echoed the environmental message in the early Sonic games, which is namely "Pollution stinks! Robotnik ain't cool!"

Here and now, winter wildfires are raging in parts of the continent that should be cool and damp until summer. Hail the size of baseballs is bashing houses, and killer tornadoes are flattening entire towns across the United States. In 2025, Hurricane Helene swept in from the Gulf of Mexico and flooded the mountains of western North Carolina, a meteorologic feat that shouldn't be possible. Gosh, all those construction paper trees and messages to "REDUCE, REUSE, RECYCLE" we cut and pasted in Grade 3 art class didn't do shit.

Everyone carries a parcel of regrets into the afterlife, and I suppose mine will be stuffed with the far-too-late realization that those cartoons, craft projects, and cheesy songs about nature turned the very serious act of saving the world into literal child's play. Talking about nature at a certain age made you sound like a dweeby tween with a home-done haircut. That was almost certainly by design. Looking back at my childhood, I really should've kicked more adults in the balls. I'm sorry.

But quite a few environmental protections were put into place around the world thanks to those shamelessly loud and insistent tween voices, and that's worth celebrating. And despite my grim outlook on humanity's future, my current state of perpetual low key despair has sharpened my affinity with '90s games that delivered serious messages about preservation. No slogans, no songs, no silly jokes or sketches.

Secret of Mana is one of those games. It shows you examples of kings and emperors draining the power of Mana for fleeting, frivolous purposes like heating a tropical resort or converting an entire city into gold. The world teeters on the edge of an environmental disaster, and the rich and powerful shrug their shoulders and declare their intent to ride the pony until it gives out from under them. Gee. *Gee*, that sounds familiar!

When I first played *Secret of Mana*, I wasn't well-versed enough with media to understand the "You Maniacs, You Blew it Up" trope, i.e. "This wreckage proves we were on Earth all along." I was fascinated when *Secret of Mana* revealed to me that the "ancient civilization" the game's introduction speaks of, the very same ancient civilization that was annihilated after it went too far and built the deadly Mana Fortress, was us. Modern humans. But the revelatory moment isn't spoken out loud. Instead, you piece the scenario together by yourself when Randi and his friends visit a sunken continent and happen upon a most unusual dungeon outfitted with lights, tile floors, turnstiles, and still-running subway trains packed with undead creatures. And by the time you reach this point in the adventure, Randi's world teeters on the lip of yet another apocalypse. Nobody's there to tell you the stakes are high, but boy, you'd better believe the stakes are high.

You'd also better believe *Secret of Mana* had an immeasurable effect on me as a writer and gamer. First and foremost, it taught me how to love RPGs again, and it was the stepping stone to a lifelong appreciation for the genre. It took me longer to realize *Secret of Mana* is also stuffed with quiet commentary about our path as a species, a topic that deserves to be explored by video games as much as any other artistic medium. It's accepted there are certain books you should read if you're an aspiring writer, and I'd argue there are some games you should play, too. *Secret of Mana* uses its graphics and music to augment a story about preservation, perseverance, and the tragedies that inevitably accompany joy — and vice-versa.

I admit I waved off *Secret of Mana*'s "simple" story as I got into RPGs with thicker narratives, e.g. the Final Fantasy games. But as I age (which I don't recommend), I appreciate more and more how this buggy, problem-ridden action RPG set me on a journey that doesn't end with celebrations, character love-ins, weddings, and triumphant fanfares.

You also beat up Santa Claus, who is a boss monster. It's, uh, a commentary on late capitalism's graveyard spiral.

CHAPTER 5

Blue is the Most Introspective Colour

"'X' possesses great risks as well as great possibilities. I can only hope for the best." - Dr. Thomas Light, *Mega Man X*

In the '80s my parents often vacationed out of the city, far away from cable access. I have dim memories of catching episodes of *Astro Boy* on those excursions thanks to an unfurled coat hanger antenna that jutted out of the window of our cabin. The antenna didn't poke out anyone's eye, but my eye *was* caught by Osamu Tezuka's timeless story about a heroic robot boy who rips ass to propel himself through the sky. And if you didn't want to watch *Astro Boy* on the coat hanger box that looked like Samara Morgan's vacation home, you could pick up a broadcast of Oopsie Daisy, a clown from Detroit. So *Astro Boy* it was.

Astro Boy is a timeless work of fiction across anime and manga. Osamu Tezuka is known as the God of Manga in Japan; modern manga and anime still owe a great deal to his pioneering works like Jungle Emperor Leo (a series about a young lion named Kimba that may or may not have "inspired" Disney's *The Lion King*), Black Jack (a series about a rogue doctor —

Tezuka studied medicine before he decided to make mangas), and Phoenix (a saga about life, death, and resurrection, and was Tezuka's unfinished opus).

Despite the fact that Tezuka's name doesn't command the same level of awe here in North America as it does in Japan, Astro Boy is instantly recognizable in wider western pop culture. Astro Boy's enduring visage in North America is probably owed to the dub of the '80s anime: The first episode of *Astro Boy* opens with a little boy named Toby getting bodied in a traffic accident after he has an argument with his father. That's not something you easily forget seeing as a kid when you're just flipping through channels in search of *Sesame Street.*

Toby's father, the grief-stricken genius scientist Dr. Umataro Tenma, engineers a replacement for his squashed son: An invulnerable robot boy who is bristling with finger-lasers and butt-guns. (What's that expression? "Men will build killer surrogate robot children before they go to therapy?")

Mecha-Toby doesn't know his own strength, nor is he perfect at emulating human behaviour, which results in a lot of accidents and property damage. This continually earns the ire of Dr. Tenma, who disowns the robot boy as his son after an especially messy dinner with a high society prima donna. (The monocle-popping "Well, I *never!*" type.) Dr. Tenma regrets his harsh words, but his robot son is bot-napped and spirited away to a robot circus before they can find each other again. Man, that is a *lot* for a premiere episode!

In retrospect I didn't spend a lot of my vacation time watching *Astro Boy.* I preferred to be on the beach slinging wet sand at my brothers when I thought the lifeguard wasn't looking. But I'd seen enough for a seed to be planted in my developing writer's mind, and it made all the difference a little further down the road.

My piqued interest in Astro Boy's intertwining of humanity and robot life drew me to Mega Man. The Mega Man series debuted as "Rockman" on the Famicom in 1987, and was promptly localized as "Mega Man" on the NES. If you can brave the Hellmouth that masquerades as *Mega Man*'s North American box art, you'll find a side-scrolling action game that's still competent but plenty frustrating.

Mega Man holds a kernel of a story that's now legendary despite how slight it is. It goes like this: Two scientists were racing for the good of all mankind. Both of them side by side, so determined—

Pardon. Couldn't resist.

Astro Boy's influence on Mega Man's story is obvious even though the first game barely has enough text to fill a book page. Mega Man and Astro Boy are both mentored by kindly scientists who view them as children, though it takes a little time for Astro to find a home with roboticist Dr. Hiroshi Ochanomizu. Dr. Ochanomizu believes in a world where robots and humans live in peace. His dream is echoed in the Mega Man series by Doctor Light, the roboticist who built the blue-armoured robot boy. Meanwhile, Dr. Tenma seethes on the cynical, dark side of Astro Boy's story, though his "asshole" stat varies between the series' many reboots and adaptations.

Dr. Wily is Dr. Tenma's analogue in the Mega Man series. He's primarily driven by a deep jealousy of Dr. Light, his former friend and research partner. Wily isn't as complicated as Dr. Tenma, but he's not without intrigue. As Dr. Light struggles at the end of his life to build Mega Man X — Mega Man's successor and the champion meant to defend the future — Dr. Wily works on his own opus: A crimson robot with unmistakably long blonde hair. Capcom rarely puts Dr. Wily and Zero in the same room, unlike how it makes it clear Dr. Light created X, but there's zero(!) doubt that Dr. Wily built the most popular character in the Mega Man fandom.

Mega Man 11's prologue adds some welcome depth to the Mega Man canon. But the vanilla struggle of Man vs. Machine that forms the bedrock of *Mega Man* was a solid story foundation as far back as 1987. Mega Man's fathers, Capcom game designers Akira Kitamura and Keiji Inafune, quickly built up a world where Mega Man is forced to confront his morals and the nature of his existence. The Robot Master bosses you fight in *Mega Man* aren't just randos cobbled together by Dr. Wily. Each one is a helper robot that Dr. Light built, and the jealous Dr. Wily subsequently corrupted. Mega Man is forced to fight his siblings, which puts a tragic twist on the Blue Bomber's quest for everlasting peace.

The classic Mega Man games give story-hunters a lot of great content to chew on. Like *Castlevania 3*, most of *Mega Man 3*'s story and world building is implied rather than explained, and the story hooks sank into me with ease. The Mega Man series' narrative about robots struggling with their identities means as much to me as its classic action mechanics and its cool Robot Masters. (Snake Man, my beloved.)

Many questions came to the fore of my mind when I played *Mega Man 3*, and a surprising number were based around robot sociology rather than physics or engineering. My biggest question was whether or not a robot could fall in love. (One of the consequences of being 11.) *Mega Man 3* doesn't answer that, but the game does have a story thread that suggests robots like Mega Man can have strong familial ties, and that was enough to keep my attention at the time.

Mega Man 3 introduces Proto Man, also known as Blues. Blues is Dr. Light's "firstborn" son. He left Dr. Light not long after he was constructed and now prefers to do lone wolf junk. Proto Man has his own mysterious reasons for keeping Mega Man at arm's length, and most of those reasons stem from the fact Proto Man is probably a shout-out to *Speed Racer*'s mysterious "Racer X" character. Racer X watches over Speed from the shadows, just as Proto Man watches Mega Man. Both Proto Man and Racer X throw dangerous challenges at their brothers to help them get stronger, or to "test them" (i.e. they want to wrestle for shits and giggles, as siblings do). It is also worth mentioning that Proto Man and Racer X both wear their sunglasses at night.

There's something magical about encountering your first anime archetype. Proto Man became *the* reason for me to play through subsequent Mega Man games. I needed to know everything about him. What was he like? Was he friends with any humans? Why is he so distant from Mega Man? Would he ever reveal the secrets hiding behind his opaque eyes and crooked smile?

Same as I was old enough to start understanding what constitutes good storytelling, I was also old enough to learn that writers will disappoint you more often than not. I struggled to overcome *Mega Man 4* (that final boss fight where Wily just straight-up turns invisible is some real horse shit), but I persevered and won. I waited for Proto Man to approach Mega Man/me and spill every drop of tea he had sloshing around in his silvery shell. I got zip. Mega Man just hitches a train home in *Mega Man 4*'s ending, and it's pretty, but anticlimactic.

"Anticlimactic" actually describes 95% of NES endings. Game endings are held to a much higher standard now, but the treats that exhausted NES game developers handed out with the credits were wild. You could usually look forward to a flaccid "Congratulation", or even a doubly-insulting "Congraduration." But I felt like *Mega Man 4* owed me the ending I wanted because *Mega Man 3* set up a great story hook. I was aghast when *Mega Man 4* didn't continue the dramatic brother saga we'd embarked on mere months ago. Why even mention Proto Man's relationship with Mega Man in the *first* place?

As pissy as those terrible endings made me, they were good for my imagination in the long run. I turned lemons into combustible lemons by tailoring epic game story conclusions in my head. Once I started thinking about how I would write those endings myself, my brain spiraled with possibilities. Most of those possibilities involved Proto Man because he was just so freakin' *cool*. I try to remember that whenever a show or a video game story makes me say "*Again* with the Seven Deadly Sins" out loud. Yeah, I've watched the metaphor get beaten to death with a wet sack of beef, but I'm middle aged. Right now some kid is seeing Proto Man for the first time in their lives, and they think he's a cool and awesome robot. And he *is* a cool and awesome robot. I still think he fits the "watcher from afar" role perfectly. I was disappointed when he didn't show up in 2018's *Mega Man 11*. I think the mysterious robot adds a special spark to the series. He belongs there as much as his blue brother. Let's hope Proto Man's faulty atomic core doesn't blow up before we get a chance to hang out with him again. That would suck.

The '90s are infamous for producing a pile of garbage game mascots that nobody remembers anymore save Gen-Xers who like to buy trash for ironic reasons. But Mega Man's leap from 8- to 16-bits was sleek and graceful. Capcom admits it had a little trouble re-designing Mega Man for the SNES, but illustrator Hayato Kaji nailed the blue robot's design by simply doing the least. When Mega Man X debuted in 1993's titular *Mega Man X,* he looked very much like the NES action hero we practically considered family by that point. But X's serious eyes and quiet nature make it clear he is not Mega Man; he's a different warrior altogether.

My time with the sometimes-grim natured Proto Man had left me well-prepared for an encounter with this '90s iteration of Mega Man. Imagine being me, circa age 13. Imagine me, someone who is already obsessed with Mega Man's portrayal of human/robot relationships, finding out Mega Man aged alongside me and was now capable of delivering a story with complexity and maturity. I *freaked.* (On the inside. My social survival instincts compelled me to bottle up my enthusiasm — I'd already learned that people don't want you around when you won't shut up about Nintendo characters.) The Mega Man games had always asked questions about sentient machinery's place amongst humanity, but those stories were framed with a little boy robot and a mad scientist. Kids' stuff, I scoffed. *Mega Man X* doesn't simply ask, "What if a bad person tried to take over the world with robots?" It asks, "What would happen if we humans, in our hubris, invented our own end? What if we were cut down by the very soldiers we'd built to protect us?"

Mega Man X is Dr. Light's opus — a robot who can think, feel genuine emotions, and decide right versus wrong without the restrictive programming of Issac Asimov's Rules of Robotics. Therein lies the rub of X's existence. The number one Rule of Robotics, "A robot must never harm a human being," is kind of a biggie. What happens when you build a robot who can wave off that rule with the casual recklessness of a teenager breaking their curfew? If X decided to go cuckoo for Cocoa Puffs and started to punch a bunch of human babies in the face, who could possibly stop him? Most robots in the Mega Man universe are built for heavy jobs, and are therefore many times more powerful than the humans they assist. Robots are beings of iron and steel; humans are just bags of bones and blood. X could theoretically turn a road rage incident into a massacre.

We learn Dr. Light planned for this eventuality. He was close to death when he finished X, but he had no one to succeed him and stand guard while the prototype robot's advanced thinky parts underwent 30 years of intensive testing. This suggests Dr. Light never got married or otherwise found a way to produce an heir. That's a shame, and kind of surprising. Capcom likes to dress Dr. Light in Ryu's *Street Fighter* gi from time to time, and rest assured the man is built.

Mega Man X's hibernation capsule and the ruins of Dr. Light's lab are excavated 100 years later by a paleontologist named Dr. Cain. Dr. Light's last son is still a miracle of robotics even a century after his conception. Dr. Cain breaks out his monkey wrench and whips up a "Reploid," a thinking-feeling robot based on X's design. But Dr. Light's blueprints for X prove baffling, and Dr. Cain majored in ancient plants, not robotics. He alters the code for his Reploid as necessary, presumably bypassing the important stuff that gifted X with his gentle, human-adjacent soul.

Unsurprisingly, Dr. Cain's hack job quickly causes a worrying number of Reploids to bug out and kill humans. In response, Dr. Cain makes his own opus, a Reploid named "Sigma." Sigma is charged with leading the "Maverick Hunters," the world's coolest name for a task force. Dr. Cain assures the world Sigma is impervious to glitches, flaws, and viruses. So of course the huge bald mother flips his electric shit and declares war on humanity.

Mega Man X's influences aren't hard to pick up. The 1982 sci-fi classic *Blade Runner* is populated by "Replicants," complex androids that are indistinguishable from humans save for their immense strength. 1985's *Terminator* is all about humanity's biggest whoopsie, i.e. inventing machines to protect us, only for them to soft-lock in a logic loop and declare humanity's only real threat is itself. Therefore, rat-a-tat-tat-tat you human scum. *Mega Man X*'s story may be kludged together by bits of '80s pop culture, but when I experienced it for the first time it was all new content. I was a bit too young to appreciate *Blade Runner* or *Terminator*. I was a soft child, not nearly hard-boiled enough to look at Kyle Reese's naked bum.

When I think back to how much *Mega Man X*'s story excited me, I also think about tropes, cliches, "overused genres," and other terms that discourage people from even writing down their basic ideas. "Who cares about this story? It's been done." It sure has! Your job is to leave your own mark on the familiar.

And I learned how to do so, given time. *Mega Man X*'s story doesn't rip off *Terminator* word for word, scene for scene. Yes, the core story is "Oh No, Robots," which doesn't sound like a big deal in a two-sentence pitch. But *Mega Man X*'s story had just the right amount of tension and drama for a novice storyteller like myself to chew over. What happens when a peaceful robot is forced to fight his own kind in the name of preserving the human race? *Terminator* observes the human-machine conflict through humans' eyes; *Mega Man X* observes it through the eyes of a robot whose blueprints are technically responsible for sparking the apocalypse. Thus the over-chewed "humans versus robots" genre still manages to split into two very different, very engaging stories. It's not inaccurate to say *Mega Man X* is one of the main pieces of media that made me realize that the sooner you accept there's nothing new under the sun, the happier you'll be as a writer. (NOTE: I cannot legally guarantee writers will ever feel anything resembling happiness, warmth, contentment, or fulfillment.)

Mega Man X also has Zero, X's senpai on the battlefield. Zero is the X series' analogue to Proto Man. His striking red armour stands out from X's humble blue work clothes, plus he has a long, blonde ponytail that chases his expert movements like a flame. Whatever else you can say about Inafune (and any Mega Man fan will say a *lot*), the man knows how to design a character that's just effin' neato. If *Mega Man X*'s mature themes weren't enough to convince me I'd found my new religion, Zero's presence compounded my fascination by multitudes. He slips in and out of the game's narrative to perform significant feats like saving X from certain death when the rookie gets in over his head. He also vanishes to perform recon while X fights the eight Maverick reploids wreaking havoc on the world. You'd think the latter job is better for an experienced Maverick Hunter like Zero, but whatever. The important thing is he comes back just long enough to feed himself to the first boss guarding Sigma's fortress. More accurately, he leaps onto its back and overloads his systems to take it out. The manoeuvre successfully demolishes the boss, *but at what cost*?

I'm now old enough to understand that mentors in Japanese media practically say "hello" by self-destructing to save their charges' lives. The trope was new to me at the time, however, and was therefore a stab to the gut and a spark in my brain. Mega Man X's universe and characters intrigued me to the point that I started thinking up stories whenever I got bored. Oh, the sins we committed to keep ourselves occupied before the days of cellphones.

It was also the days before schoolkids tapped out their assignments on computers. We were taught how to write using newsprint, pens, pencils, and agonizing repetition. Boomers are still over the moon for cursive writing, but it was a source of misery for me as a kid. I was scolded, told to slow down, to stop being careless, and was constantly docked marks for neatness. I don't blame the teachers; nobody was paying them a fortune to decipher my chicken scratch, let alone grade it. But the scolding did take a lot of fun out of writing. Plus, the actual act of writing physically hurt me. I had trouble holding writing tools, and I tended to bear down on my pencil with the intensity of a woman giving birth. My motor skills simply sucked, perhaps because I'm cross-dominant. (i.e. I use different hands for different tasks. I write with my right hand, but I play many sports with my left hand.)

Worse, the physical discomfort of writing merged with my long-lasting fear of litigious game companies. I neglected to write my story ideas down because I still believed that the fanfic police would knock on my door the second I scrawled "Mega Man X" on a sheet of paper.

That changed by the mid-90s when I took a serious typing class in high school. I only knew how to hunt-and-peck thanks to my elementary school's Apple][programs that commanded us to type "Debbie Does Dirty Dishes" over and over. (I'm serious.) My typing teacher was a small and severe lady who once got into a fight with my grade 9 math teacher (her husband) during class. She taught us on typewriters and we got marks off for every mistake made. I secretly called her the Viking, and given her tiny stature, I don't know why. She wasn't my favourite teacher, but I admit her Type or Die method of teaching proved effective. Being able to type my stories brought back my joy of writing because I could finally put my thoughts down as quickly as they formed.

That spring, an acquaintance from the Planet Nerd sector of my high school asked me to attend a meeting about the joys of being online. I had no idea what "being online" meant, but apparently our school was one of the first in the province to get an online hook-up, so it was a big deal.

I attended the meeting out of courtesy. By the time summer rolled around, I was stumbling through every slummy fan page web 1.0 could possibly offer me at glorious 56k. Discovering the internet was like suddenly throwing open a door and finding a sprawling realm where I could finally be *heard*. None of my school friends really wanted to talk about video games with me, and hoo boy, was I corked right up. Early fandom was already taking shape in the pale digital dawn, and I easily found websites about Final Fantasy, Sonic the Hedgehog, and the jackpot, the game-changer: proto-message boards all about Mega Man and Mega Man X. After a long, awkward journey through an analogue age, I'd finally broken through humankind's physical limits and found My People. My weird, weird, people.

I discovered fanfiction not long after I began surfin' the net. Back then, people sent in stories to the webmasters of the tiny fan sites, and said webmaster formatted the story for HTML by hand and posted it to a "library" hosted somewhere on their page. We were some years away from a centralized hub like Fanfiction.net, so these webmasters were writers' only hope for being published and seen.

I was stunned, maybe even scandalized, at how flagrantly Mega Man X fanfictions lay around in plain sight like nude sunbathers. Was this even *allowed*? Were all these stories approved by Capcom? Surely they had to be! How else could they be permitted to exist?

I had no way of knowing fanfic was indeed considered a legal threat in some fandoms. Authors like Anne McCaffrey and Anne Rice ordered fans to stay away from the Pern and Vampire Chronicles properties respectively. But their battles were fought (and subsequently lost) in fandoms I didn't follow, and therefore never visited in the digital realm. Capcom, Nintendo, Sega, and Squaresoft were living their own lives in Japan and could therefore care less if a bunch of weird westerners wanted to make Locke Cole from *Final Fantasy VI* kiss Knuckles the Echidna with tongue. In that way, the internet already contained parallels to the real world: I found myself in a calm country that afforded me a lot of creative freedom, oblivious to ongoing wars in other realms. Some fans had to scratch and bite and burrow underground for the right to write about Barbie dragons, and meanwhile I was on the verge of watching my favourite characters get wrecked over and over again by authors of variable skill and sanity. I was truly alive.

About half the Mega Man fanfiction and fanart available at the time featured Zero instead of Mega Man X, the theoretical star of the series. Zero's popularity in the west also received a rocket-powered boost thanks to the ending of 1995's *Mega Man X3*, which was the most recent Mega Man X release at the time I first got online. As Mega Man X and Zero gaze over the ruins of their battle in *X3*'s finale, the accompanying text crawl informs us that "In order to save mankind, X must destroy Zero." Not long after *Mega Man X3*'s release, someone, somewhere found and shared a rare tidbit from Japan that explained the reason why: Just as Mega Man X was Dr. Light's final creation, Zero was Dr. Wily's final creation. Like, holy shit. How is that *not* going to make us scatterbrained little weasels run for the nearest keyboard and start rolling all over it?

Again, the Mega Man X games run on themes more than singular stories. They ask us to consider how beings of metal can live peacefully alongside beings of flesh. They ask us to consider what the world would be like if humankind inadvertently invented the tools of its own destruction. And now the games were asking "Yoooo, what if, like, Zero was built by Dr. Wily, like X was built by Dr. Light? Isn't that shit *wild*?"

This new intrigue surrounding Zero made the Mega Man X universe a huge draw for fanfic writers who appreciated the series' serious themes. The games' sparse narrative also offered a lot of creative wiggle room, so those early fanfics tended to be bloodier and more violent than Capcom's intent. We were all at the perfect age for piling more misery upon Mega Man X, as if the poor prototype reploid wasn't agonized enough.

Shadow the Hedgehog did not yet exist to guide us through our turbulent tweens and early teens, so we had to make do with stories about Reploids (and often humans) being chopped up, destroyed, and tormented.

These fanfics also weren't very good, truth be told. Like the works of Vonnegut's deranged persona Kilgore Trout, they were great ideas wrapped in amateurish writing. That's not a slight against the stories' authors. I'm sure they'd agree with me: 16-year-olds are shitty writers. That's okay. It's teenagers' job to write shitty things, tear themselves down, and learn how to get a handle on their voice.

Reading fanfiction made me less apprehensive about writing it. No mass arrests had occurred in the Mega Man fandom. I figured I was safe. I *was* safe. I couldn't say the same for the souls who subsequently received my first Mega Man X fanfiction, chapter by chapter, over email, and then live on a major fan website. It was a whorl of chaos that attracted fellow beings of disarray.

My first fans. O God. How terrifying.

I will hand myself this much: The story was unlike anything anyone had written up until that point. In grade 6 I wrote a hilarious mess of a Super Mario fanfiction as part of a class project. (I figured it wasn't plagiarism if it was schoolwork, and thankfully, my teacher agreed.) The ridiculous misfortunes that befell poor Mario and Luigi had made my class laugh uproariously, which is primo energy when you're an extroverted introvert like me who wants to disappear into the background while being the centre of attention.

I wanted to make people laugh again, because heck, I also loved laughing with and at my heroes. I couldn't take the act of writing fanfiction any more seriously than I take anything in life, so my own version of Zero's revision to his primal Maverick form was incredibly stupid.

I think I also believed on a subconscious level that I could shield myself with humour. People are less likely to point out ridiculous plot holes when they're busy laughing.

I set the story directly after the events of *Mega Man X3*, which was the style at the time. Post-*X3* stories usually involve Zero succumbing to the darkness that awakens within and orders him to peel Mega Man X like a ripe fruit. My dilemma was my warring desires to make people laugh while also indulging in *X3*'s story potential. I did my best to combine the two, but at the end of the day we were still talking about oil and water.

It was common for fanfic writers to whip up stories about the Mavericks triggering Zero's dark side as opposed to waiting for it to come out naturally. That's the direction I went in. There is a scene in my story where Zero is incapacitated and captured by the Mavericks, who have been secretly gathering their strength since their last defeat. Zero's kidnapping is overseen by a Maverick named Vile, a recurring villain in the Mega Man X series. The chapter that builds up to Zero being turned against the Maverick Hunters still has its goofs and laffs but the tone is notably more serious than in chapters where Mega Man X and Zero yelled at each other, cracked jokes, and broke shit. Vile tells the captive Zero his reason for wanting to purge the planet of the human race: Humans, cursed by heredity, were doomed to die in a long struggle to remain as Earth's dominant species against the perfect Reploids, so why not hurry things along by making Zero the Maverick he was always intended to be?

This honestly intriguing conversation was preceded by a scene wherein Zero and Mega Man X get into a fight while travelling to the Mavericks' secret base in a multi-seater Ride Armour. (A Ride Armour is a mecha-suit X can jump into to expand his power – there are several in Sting Chameleon's stage in *Mega Man X*. I invented a new one called the Gryphon for the purpose of the story and property destruction.) The argument builds to a red-hot point until an enraged Zero rips X's *Pulp Fiction* CD out of the Gryphon's CD drive and throws it out the window like a tiny silver frisbee. Zero then departs the vehicle and strikes out on his own, which is coincidentally how he gets caught by Vile.

I don't know what to tell you. Why *Pulp Fiction*? Because, to echo internet comedian Kevin James Thornton, *"It was the Nine-teeeeees~!"* I'd never thrown anyone's CD or tape out of a moving vehicle but I'd heard stories from other delinquents. And I thought, "Man, it would suck if your friend threw something you loved out the car window. But the visual is also really funny." Zero's act of throwing a *Pulp Fiction* CD out of a hulking mech elevates the scene's tension, but the whole thing is so ridiculous that you can't help but laugh.

(Sidenote: I grew up on DiC's *Super Mario Bros. 3* cartoon adaptation. There is an episode wherein Mario and Luigi get into a fight that climaxes with Luigi throwing Mario's "hot" record on the fire and declaring "There, now it's even hotter!" I still think that scene is funny and there is an excellent chance I was thinking about it when I wrote my own work of art.)

I admittedly like to think I have a talent for using humour to hit the steam valve pressure release whenever in-story events get dark. There's a trick to it, and it can be a delicate operation. But teen writers aren't good with "delicate." Mega Man X and Zero's Angry *Pulp Fiction* Adventure (not the fanfic's real name) was basically me trying to make comedy and drama stick together like cold lumps of plasticine. I had a lot to learn. I was a toddler.

I don't have kids, but I know that toddlers never shut up. I don't say that to be mean, I actually think it's fascinating to watch the little imps gawp unblinkingly at their parents as they're bombarded with words, gestures, and social cues. Human communication is exceptionally complicated. It takes a lot of effort to learn the bare basics like "Don't pick your nose and wipe it on my bicycle shorts." That's one reason why toddlers love to yell and shriek, usually in the part of the grocery store where the largest number of people can gather and judge you. They need you to acknowledge their voice! Acknowledge their right to exist in this world and dump apple juice onto expensive carpets!

Young writers are loud and clumsy in the same way. My earliest fanfics were me working through my toddler-hood and gradually learning how to control my voice. There is a time for levity, and a time for drama. A writer can learn how to make the two moods compliment each other, but I was essentially banging pots and pans together until I learned that skill for myself.

I still enjoy writing Mega Man fanfiction. I haven't published all of it — there are a lot of unfinished scraps squirreled away in old hard drives — but it's an easy property to build upon and experiment with because I'm so familiar with it. It's ignoble to call Mega Man my practice dummy, but that's what it's been since I started to take writing seriously over three decades ago.

I still have a copy of my premiere 'fic, but I'm going to have to beg your pardon and refrain from publishing it here. You know when you give birth to your first child and it's a hideous mutant that *kind* of mirrors your phenotype just enough to spark your protective instincts? But you know this child of yours is a Thing That Cannot be Touched By the Sun, so you lock it away for its own good, even though you still see so very much of yourself in that sagging, grey face? That's me and my first fanfic. I am happy it exists, even if it's just a shade on the internet now. My genetic code is still in that mess. It's the reason I became brave enough to consider writing as a career.

Thank you, Mega Man, for equipping me with writing, which in turn equipped me with some semblance of everlasting peace.

CHAPTER 6

Drop Everything, Here Comes Final Fantasy VI

"I don't care for the appearance of this pitiful little hamlet... So burn it!"
- Kefka, *Final Fantasy VI*

Final Fantasy VI — localized in North America as *Final Fantasy III* because several Final Fantasy games were no-shows on our shores in 1994 — was the first video game to treat me like an adult. It was also the first game that taught me how to write like an adult. Titles like *Mega Man X* and *Secret of Mana* flirt with heavy topics like robot racism and death, but *Final Fantasy VI* is not a shonen-style adventure or even a dark fairy tale. It's about the world being enveloped by a literal mad clown who doubles as an agent of pure hatred and chaos. The people (and heroes) caught up in the darkness are forced to consider if there's any point to fighting, to living.

Most of *Final Fantasy VI*'s characters shout out "Yes!" with great conviction. But a shocking number of characters choose to fade into the poisoned landscape. *Final Fantasy VI* champions humanity's talent for scratching for light wherever it can be found, but it also reminds us the fight is not easy. People die. People break. Yet after facing innumerable hardships that

I didn't even know were allowed to exist in a video game, *Final Fantasy VI*'s large cast of characters finally manage to climb to the top of Mount Clown and state the reasons why they decide to keep on living despite Kefka's attempts to snuff out their flames again and again.

The scene taught me the power of people's resilience. And the power of a good old-fashioned anime love-in. Why do people fight to live? Because the alternative is to fade, and not everyone is ready to do that. When those are your options, as is the case with the diminished population living in *Final Fantasy VI*'s magic-blasted wasteland, you make your choice and live with it — or don't live with it, as the case may be. But those who choose to stay and fight, like *Final Fantasy VI*'s cast, still find embers of hope buried under the ashen earth. And over the next 40 hours, we learn even the smallest sparks can drive back the deepest darkness.

Despite being one of the darkest RPGs of its time, *Final Fantasy VI* was prepped for release during Nintendo of America's notoriously puritanical era. *Mortal Kombat*'s violence was causing parents' monocles to pop off in horror, so Nintendo courted aghast adults with promises of "family friendly" games. Among a host of other rules, SNES games could no longer reference death. Squaresoft game localizer Ted Woolsey was expected to convey the angst and agony of this crumbling world without using terms like "dying" or "die." But for all the tampering done to make *Final Fantasy VI*'s script safe for '90s kid consumption, the game never talks down to its audience. I think kids' media was over-regulated in the '90s, but I also believe those limits sharpened creators and made them more determined to ensure we weren't fed pure pablum.

Final Fantasy VI's legacy is augmented by its rich presentation. The adventure guides you through scenery that's still worth writing stories about. The size and detail of Yoshitaka Amano's monsters are, as always, brilliant and beautiful. There are still compromises that are expected from cartridge games from the age: *Final Fantasy VI*'s character sprites are noticeably simple compared to the near-photorealistic backgrounds they appear against. Otherwise, *Final Fantasy VI* is one of the best-looking games on the SNES. It shows off sparkly magical effects that make smart use of the SNES' ability to scale and rotate sprites. The characters boast magic and skills that rain liquid fire, freeze foes into huge columns of ice, or shake the screen to simulate atomic blasts. *Final Fantasy VI*'s most powerful spell, "Ultima," cleanses the entire screen under a dome of electric blue light that grows, grows, grows, and then explodes in a final flash of white. It's reminiscent of the dome-like explosion that flash-fries Tokyo in the classic 1988 anime action movie *Akira.* To think that a video game, an RPG no less, was capable of emulating such an iconic moment of animation history. Just mind-boggling.

Final Fantasy VI's graphics also wordlessly illustrate the cultures occupying each corner of the world. In the north, there is a prosperous desert kingdom full of people hustling and bustling between medieval-style structures. A nearby mining town tucked inside a cave is threaded with steaming pipes that keep citizens warm and machinery running. Across the ocean, the Empire has subjugated a continent by twisting magic and tech. The unholy union makes for its own grim aesthetic, which the Empire carries into each town it smashes. In between all that, thieves thrive in a broken-down town, and an opera house shows off the more opulent, cultural side of the world's population. *Final Fantasy VI* is a visual miracle.

It's also a miracle of sound. Final Fantasy series composer Nobuo Uematsu pushes the SNES sound chip to a near-meltdown with *Final Fantasy VI*'s 60+-song soundtrack. The catalogue's crowning achievement is "Aria di Mezzo Carattere," an interactive opera song that *Final Fantasy VI*'s cast uses to lure a gambling rogue into their grasp. Hey, when you need to get a dude's attention so you can bargain for use of his airship, you need to do whatever is necessary.

The entire sequence surrounding "Aria di Mezzo Carattere" was jarring the first time I experienced it. I was still a little shaky with turn-based RPG mechanics when I first played *Final Fantasy VI*, and going from beating up giant hornets and angry cats to directing a digital opera performance was initially overwhelming. To my credit, console RPGs had never tried anything as grand as a whole story sequence built around a theatre show. I was just starting to realize video games' potential as a story vessel, but Squaresoft was far ahead of me.

Instead of having us read story text on a screen, the story of Aria di Mezzo Carattere is sung to us by a little blonde sprite who's performing her heart out. Your job as the player is twofold: One, you must make sure she sings the right lines, which you select as they pop up along with the song. Second, you must stymie the recurring octopus villain named Ultros as he attempts to, quote, "jam up your opera."

When I rewatch *Final Fantasy VI*'s opera sequence, I'm still moved by its mash-up of performance and gameplay, of drama and comedy. I also recall how strange it was to experience it for the first time in an era without widespread internet, social media, guides, or any other way for me to suss out these strange new storytelling mechanics outside of trial and error. My first obstacle was picking out the proper lines to sing. This isn't a hard task if you have a sensible head on your shoulders: It simply requires you to memorize a very short song script that you can access before the show. From there, you select the proper song prompt for each verse. If, however, your brain hemispheres maybe don't fire in tandem so good, you might be forced to write down the opera script in its entirety just to make sure you don't select the wrong prompts. (That said, some of the mistakes are pretty funny. One screwed-up line sees the singer belt out "Prince Ralse? I hate him. Everyone does." So melodious.)

The opera does offer some moments of traditional combat, albeit in a non-traditional setting. Ultros' efforts to sabotage the performance bear evil fruit, and Aria di Mezzo Carattere becomes Gong Show di Mezzo Carattere. Saving the day involves climbing up to the rafters, beating back the diseased rats nesting there, and then battling Ultros in the slimy flesh to the accompaniment of a whole-ass orchestral movement that you never hear anywhere else in the game. Only *then* does the owner of the coveted airship notice you, which takes you one step closer to securing his craft for your needs.

It's an astoundingly well-directed sequence, not to mention a memorable break from the usual grind. I was already familiar with the RPG trope of doing something significant to earn a swift means of transport, but it usually involved fighting a tough enemy or going on a grand quest to collect MacGuffins that awaken a legendary mount. *Final Fantasy VI*'s subquest to recruit the Blackjack airship through a literal singing and dancing routine was unprecedented. It sure taught me a few things about how RPG mechanics can change on a dime when the story determines a target can't be overcome with brute strength alone.

For all of *Final Fantasy VI*'s grandiosity, it still offers quiet, contemplative moments of character development that I was too hopped-up on Pepsi to appreciate in the '90s. The opera itself is a veritable layer cake of story development that projects the problematic love between two of *Final Fantasy VI*'s main characters: Locke Cole and Celes Chere. (The aforementioned opera floozy who's doing her best.) Locke, the party's thief — ahem, *treasure hunter* — archetype, presents as a cheerful, carefree adventurer. Truthfully, he's haunted by the memory of an accident and a subsequent Imperial attack that stole his lover, Rachel, from him. Locke blames himself for the accident, and appeals to his home village's resident kook for herbs to keep Rachel's corpse from decomposing. Locke's goal in life is to find the Empire's "legendary treasure," a mysterious device that's said to be able to call wandering souls back to their body.

Yeah, Locke is a deeply effed-up individual who's keeping his dead girlfriend on ice long enough to bring her back to life. This detail is not missed by Celes, a stone-hearted former Imperial General who starts warming up to Locke after her Opera performance brings them closer. Celes clearly wants to get to know Locke better, but she's rightfully worried that if they become a couple, he'll slip up and call her "Rachel" in bed. As for Locke, he carries faint but noticeable doubts about Celes' allegiances given her history with the Empire that iced his girlfriend.

I called *Final Fantasy VI* the first game that treated me like an adult. The rocky relationship between Locke and Celes is a good example of what I mean. We're not talking about puppy love. We're not talking about two teenagers goofing around until they finally realize they're into each other. Locke and Celes are two adults carrying loads of baggage that need to be cleared away with a firehose before they can consider getting together. It's a very interesting dynamic to write, since most of Celes and Locke's relationship isn't directly explored or alluded to through words. Their simple gestures are shared against some of the game's most beautiful set pieces, and are designed to make your brain gibber. One of my favourite scenes in *Final Fantasy VI* happens close to the game's halfway point. The embers between the thief and the general are waning because events have bred suspicion and mistrust between them. Both are forced to go on a mission together, which requires them to stay at a village inn for a night. Locke walks out of his room in the middle of the night to confront Celes, who won't meet his gaze as she just stares down into the dark water running under the bridge below.

Locke tries to apologize for thinking Celes still holds loyalties to the Empire, but it's a bumbling attempt. Celes runs from Locke, who watches in silence as a wavering music box rendition of "Aria di Mezzo Carattere" plays in the background. You're not aware when you first hear it, but this lovely little morsel of music dedicated to Celes will intertwine with Locke's theme when the day is finally won and the cast list gets rolled out. Locke and Celes never say "I love you" to one another, but the marriage of RPG characters' personal themes feels much more intimate.

Final Fantasy VI is famous for being a game where the bad guys explicitly win. Kefka is not a normal villain, and his twisted kingdom — referred to as the "World of Ruin" on a world map that was included in *Final Fantasy VI*'s box — is not a normal apocalyptic wasteland. It's far rougher than any other post-apocalyptic setting seen in a console game to that date. It's not a dark, cyberpunk backdrop that you wander while beating people up. (Love you *Double Dragon*, mwah.) The World of Ruin's bloodied seas, ashen soil, rampant undead wildlife, and horrendous body count explicitly drive characters to attempt suicide.

Yes, Celes is so driven to despair in her first few moments of living in the World of Ruin that she tries to kill herself. To be fair, it's a rude awakening even for a battle-hardened general. Her elderly father figure Cid dies of exhaustion shortly after nursing her through her coma. (Each Final Fantasy story is allotted one [1] iteration of Cid for story purposes. Cid is usually depicted in an engineering role, but the poor old bastard doubles as a despair-inducing redshirt in *Final Fantasy VI*'s second half.) Even before Death robs Celes of the only other living human that she knows of, *Final Fantasy VI* plops you onto a radically-altered overworld tileset populated by dying creatures. Random enemy encounters on the island fetch up weakened monsters who are preemptively afflicted by the "Poison" status. As soon as the monsters line up to attack, their single hit point saps away and they die before Celes can raise her sword. Only one lifeform is thriving on the dying island: A zombified dragon that lives in its small patch of desert.

Most millennials and xillennials who grew up with *Final Fantasy VI* will recount their first visit to the World of Ruin with awe and reverence. Those of us who are honest will admit we just about shit our pants when we saw Kefka kick off the apocalypse for the first time. I thought I'd broken the game or made a wrong choice somewhere. It's neat to look back on *Final Fantasy VI*'s mid-game shift and admire how skillfully SquareSoft built it, but good writing was honestly the last thing on my mind as I tore ass through the half-game terminus. The gang's final desperate dash to the airship is preceded by a boss battle that is no joke, and if you fall to a random battle during the escape, the fight with this high-level beast happens all over again.

Even if you escape successfully, victory over the monster feels hollow because there's no way to stop the coming destruction. You don't get a chance to save until some time after you watch the world degrade into the World of Ruin, which soured the prospect of hitting the reset button and doing things the "right" way. (Again: Impossible.) The controller is in your hands for much of *Final Fantasy VI*'s apocalypse, which makes you responsible for the well-being of your party members. When everything goes tits-up, you feel frightened and remorseful. It's another example of *Final Fantasy VI* melding mediums to spice up its games' story impact.

It's chilling how purposefully alone and helpless you're made to feel when you, as Celes, take your first steps ashore on the World of Ruin's rearranged continents. It's dangerous to fight alone in any part of *Final Fantasy VI*, let alone the World of Ruin's wastelands. But that's what Celes does, often against zombified, mutated enemies who are capable of one-shotting the lone warrior by turning her into stone, or by making her a member of the undead herself. Status effects that are easily curable as long as there's another party member present become a death sentence.

Starting from rock bottom and ambling up the slow path to victory also gives *Final Fantasy VI* a chance to prove its point about the persistence and hardiness of life's primal flame. It's not a *happy* game, but it's a hopeful one that takes years to fully digest. Indeed, I made the rookie writer mistake of initially thinking *Final Fantasy VI* is "dark" for the sake of being dark, and that its journey of trauma, agony, and loss was supposed to inspire deep cynicism instead of hope. In other words, *Final Fantasy VI* was "cool," and that's all that mattered to me at the climax of the SNES vs. Sega Genesis schoolyard wars.

It's a terrible lesson to take from such an emotionally beautiful game, but it's a teenage writer's birthright to miss the point of everything before contributing to the art. It was only after many (many) replays of *Final Fantasy VI* that I came to admire how carefully it wields its despair. Terrible things happen as the World of Ruin degrades under the party's feet, but it's always paired with a flash of hope or character development. Celes finds Sabin when the monk pauses for a moment to hold up a whole-ass house that's about to collapse on a child. Sabin finds his twin brother Edgar shortly thereafter, and the two work together to save their imperiled home castle. The growing band then finds the noble samurai Cyan, who has been sending letters to a young woman to spare her the pain of learning her boyfriend was dead. (A search through his belongings also reveals he's into Bushido hentai.) Cyan conveniently decides to knock that crap off when he rejoins the party — though doing so doesn't do anything to soothe the torment he feels after losing his wife and child to the poison Kefka poured in Doma's waterways.

These interludes advance *Final Fantasy VI*'s story while letting players reconnect with its scattered cast. They also give SquareSoft the opportunity to strut its storytelling stuff. In one scenario, Celes needs to find and talk to Setzer about finding another airship so they can elbow-drop Kefka's crazy garbage tower from the air. That first hard-won airship, which required a whole opera performance to snag, was snapped like a twig during the apocalypse. Setzer leads him to the tomb of an old friend named Daryl who died when a daring airship flight went badly. The airship, called the Falcon, has been resting at the bottom of the tomb since Setzer found and restored it. As Celes and her friends follow Setzer into the depths, we see flashbacks of Setzer kidding with Daryl projected against the tomb's black wall. An acoustic rendition of Setzer's theme plays during the descent, which adds a very potent jab of melancholy into this free-spirited gambler who'd seemed unbothered by the world before it ended. It's an impressively cinematic story moment, something SquareSoft was clearly champing at the bit to do more of. (It got its chance when it switched to CD-based game development and told Nintendo and the cartridge-based N64 to fly a kite.)

Final Fantasy VI's mood lifts a little when the small party finds the Falcon. The World of Ruin isn't Disneyland, in fact it's still quite horrifying, but at least Celes now knows that she has reason to hope. The first flight of the Falcon seems almost joyful, making it a vital counter-balance to the relentless onslaught of shock and sadness belted out from the time Celes wakes up until the time the Falcon breaches the surface of the dying sea. It took some growing up as a writer before I understood *Final Fantasy VI*'s most valuable writing lesson: Themes of despair are best used carefully. If the bodies are to hit the floor, then let them hit the floor. But I'm at the age where my friends and family are starting to die from stupid, unfair, and inexplicable causes, so I have a growing appreciation for fictional character deaths that do more than simply fuel the furnace of tragedy.

Like most great stories, *Final Fantasy VI* uses smaller character-driven experiences to shepherd its larger world-saving narrative from start to finish. Locke gets his chance to say goodbye to his kind-of dead girlfriend, Rachael, who tells him in turn that he needs to stop clinging to her because living in the real world should always take precedence over mourning memories. (Rachael also suggests Locke should hook up with the person he "holds in his heart." This obviously refers to Celes, and it's sporting of Rachael to give the General a nice recc as she fades into Phoenix's bosom.) The twin brothers Sabin and Edgar resolve to work together and realize their late parents' dream of a stronger kingdom. Cyan literally fights his own demons to cleave the deep-rooted grief that's festered in him since his family was poisoned. And the wild boy Gau, who was abandoned to die on a savannah filled with monsters, learns his father still thinks he did the right thing by leaving his newborn "demon child" to its fate. Okay, *Final Fantasy VI* usually has a point when it hurts you, but sometimes it also just wants to be mean and make you cry. At least Gau gets a nice suit out of the traumatizing visit.

Two longer strands of the World of Ruin's plot spaghetti have particularly important things to say about identity, responsibility, and the bonds between the party members. But whereas one story is easy to come across through normal gameplay, the other story is literally and metaphorically hidden in the shadows.

Shadow, *Final Fantasy VI*'s resident ninja, is a loner mercenary who initially only sticks with the party for money. He can eventually be enticed into becoming a permanent party member, which is a good idea because Shadow's killer doberman Interceptor comes as part of the deal.

When you hang out with Shadow, there's a chance that sleeping at an inn will reveal one of several dream sequences that piece together Shadow's past as Clyde, a failed train robber. We learn a botched heist left Clyde and his partner in crime, Baram, badly injured. Baram, knowing he's done for, asks Clyde to kill him before he's caught and brutalized by the authorities. Clyde chickens out and runs. The final dreams imply that Clyde kept running until he collapsed in the small town of Thamasa, where he settled for a time. The dreams purposefully lack specific details — it's the nature of a dream to be vague and hazy — but they heavily suggest Clyde/Shadow is the father of Relm, *Final Fantasy VI*'s youngest party member.

"Wow, what are the odds?" you might ask. I suppose they'd be high enough in a world where memory limitations mean your game might have a hundred NPCs in total. Seriously though, I spent a lot of time thinking about Shadow's hidden past while my peers did normal human things like play sports and interact with each other.

Square has admitted in past interviews that it wants to keep the threads loose between Relm and Shadow, which is an admirable act of restraint from its narrative designers. Unsurprisingly, admirable acts of restraint weren't my forte when I was a teenage writer. I wanted to know why Clyde left baby Relm behind to go cosplay all over the world as a perpetually broke ninja. I was convinced I was missing some tell-all scene, and I held onto that belief until budding game programmers got good enough to tear apart *Final Fantasy VI*'s code and declare "nope." So I sensibly decided "That is unacceptable" and started to write my *own* story about why Clyde slipped behind Shadow's cowl.

I couldn't always write fanfiction in my school's computer lab because there was a risk someone who needed a computer for schoolwork would squeal on me and get me kicked off. I mangled the prompt with a pen and notepad because my access to computers was spotty back then. Going back to the old ways physically hurt my hand, plus I became a living Boomer joke when I despaired over my lack of undo, backspace, cut, and paste.

The end result was choppy, sloppy, and ultimately unfinished. It was the kind of thing you'd expect from a young writer attempting to untangle an unexpectedly mature theme offered to her by a video game. Again, it's not surprising that my first instinct after playing a grim game like *Final Fantasy VI* was to make drama for drama's sake. I imagined maybe Clyde left because he hated his new wife. Maybe he resented the idea of being pinned down, as he was used to being a thief and a wanderer. Maybe he was just an asshole. Shadow *did* have a habit of leaving the party high and dry, after all.

It's not an invalid scenario, but again, it's a shallow and cynical way to interpret a game as deeply hopeful as *Final Fantasy VI*. If I'd been in less of a rush to assume the worst of Clyde when I wrote my fanfic, I would have slowed down to chew over the story tidbits SquareSoft left strewn about. *Final Fantasy VI* has a relic called the "Momento Ring," which protects its wearer from instant death attacks. There are two Rings, and only two characters can wear them: Relm and Shadow. Relm is wearing one of the rings when she joins your party. The other ring can be found in the master bedroom of her house after a dramatic story sequence. Shadow stands apart from the party during the exposition dump, as ninjas are wont to do. But when you check where he was standing a little later, you'll find the second Ring. This suggests the Momento Rings are wedding rings, and that Shadow hung onto his own ring until that moment. Whoever Relm's mother was, Clyde loved her. Maybe seeing Relm alive and well was enough for him to let go. In any case, *Final Fantasy VI* never gives any indication Clyde resented settling down. In fact, it offers strong evidence that he's still mushy about his old life. If you're the type of writer who loves to stretch your observational skills, stories like Clyde's are your catnip.

Identity is also a major theme in *Final Fantasy VI,* and it's the basis for its other inspiring story beat. Terra, a mysterious girl who's only half human, must ask herself which world she belongs to. The other half of Terra's blood is credited to magical creatures called "Espers," which were used as living weapons by warring kingdoms thousands of years ago. It's no surprise Terra's wild heritage eventually inspires an existential crisis that's so devastating, it turns her into a flying screaming glam rock monster that looks like a Barbie doll. That means you're left without access to Terra as a party member until you help her come to terms with her origin.

Once in a while a video game pulls some mechanical trick that makes me say "Are they allowed to do that?" Witnessing Terra's literal flight from my party was one of those moments.

Robbing me of a major party member for story reasons is ballsy, though I appreciate the twist a lot more now than I did when I was 14. *Final Fantasy IV* shuffles characters in and out of your roster too, but the story reasons don't get complicated beyond "Well shit, Kain's left us for the bad guys again" or "Yang was adopted by Sylphs." *Final Fantasy VI* won't give Terra back until you help her come to terms with her heritage.

I have a soft spot for stories about characters who come from two explicitly different backgrounds, being of mixed heritage myself and witnessing chaotic Seders fueled by cultural discrepancies. But difficult questions aren't answered within 20 hours of gameplay. *Final Fantasy VI* robs you of Terra again in the World of Ruin to make its point. The cost of getting her back is to sit down and learn a lesson about life and love. Not every problem can be solved with swords alone. Sometimes you need introspection. And maybe one or two swords.

When Celes first undergoes her World of Ruin rescue/recruitment drive, she finds Terra in the remnants of Mobliz, a former settlement in what's arguably the most unfortunate corner of the shattered globe. When Kefka turned his wrath on Mobliz during Doomsday, the village's adults died while trying to save their kids. Terra then became a mother figure for the traumatized children left behind. Terra is 18 years old during the events of *Final Fantasy VI*, and she's the oldest adult in Mobliz. There are two others: A hot-tempered 17-year-old named Duane and his also-17 girlfriend, Katarin. The three work hard to turn their underground orphanage into a refuge for the children, but things get complicated when Duane knocks up Katarin.

When I played *Dragon Warrior* in 1990, I saved a princess from a dragon. Four years later, *Final Fantasy VI* enveloped me in an episode of "Degrassi." It's not only shocking that *Final Fantasy VI* straight up has a story where a girl gets "teen pregnant," it's shocking Nintendo of America let the scenario exist intact. Though, the original English script shoehorns in some comment about Duane and Katarin being married. The '90s were really weird about showing unmarried couples and the bastard products of said unions. When Trunks tells Goku he was the illegitimate product of a one night hate-hump between Vegeta and Bulma in a 2000 episode of "Dragon Ball Z," it marked the first time I heard a character in a kids' show admit to being born on the wrong side of the sheets. Just makes Trunks that much cooler.

In an April 2019 *Famitsu* interview translated by Japanese culture site One Million Power about *Final Fantasy VI*'s 25th anniversary, series creator Hironobu Sakaguchi revealed that he watched his daughter being born while *Final Fantasy VI* was in development, an event that understandably moved him. It's no wonder you can practically taste Sakaguchi's emotional energy in parts of *Final Fantasy VI's* narrative, and why he went as far as to have a young woman get preggers in a post-apocalyptic wasteland. It's proof of video games' power as an art form and an emotional exchange. When you feel deeply about something, you can't help but spill some of that emotion into whatever you're creating.

And like all pregnancies, Katarin's condition comes with a host of anxieties. There's no celebration when she reveals her pregnancy to Duane because, you know, bringing a kid into a world that's been turned upside-down isn't always an A+ idea. But when the two teens reconcile and try to understand what's happening to them, a demon suddenly attacks Mobliz. (*That* never happened on "Degrassi.") Terra, who found herself drained of her desire to fight after the end of the world, dons her feral half-Esper form to help Celes kill the monster. She then realizes she needs to take down Kefka if the kids of Mobliz, born and unborn alike, are to have any kind of a future. Terra then understands that her determination to fight for others so they can live peaceful lives is what love is all about.

The scenario outlines how life will even take root and blossom in terrible places. It speaks to Sakaguchi's respect for games that he allowed such a personal piece of himself to be put into *Final Fantasy VI*. The older I get, the more I appreciate how Duane, Katarin, and Terra feed a spark of potential until it becomes a flame of hope. *Final Fantasy VI* wants us to understand that no matter how dark things become, life, love, and the natural order of things will always find a way to endure. I still hold that message close to my bountiful bosom, and I have big plans to cling onto it until I die.

CHAPTER 7

Pokémon's Lessons About Nature Writing, or "All Creatures Big and Shayman"

"Strong Pokémon. Weak Pokémon. That is only the selfish perception of people. Truly skilled Trainers should try to win with the Pokémon they love best." - Karen, *Pokémon Silver*

I had a subscription to *Nintendo Power* in 1998, but only because my future husband had gifted it to me. Otherwise I never would have bothered. By that point I'd acknowledged that the N64's fortunes were looking kind of dismal next to Sony's PlayStation upstart. (But not as bad as the Sega Saturn, whose utter trampling in North America is a tale of woe.)

Nintendo Power was mostly a morass of blurry brown screenshots in those days outside of small peeks of sunshine from previews of *The Legend of Zelda: Ocarina of Time*. But the gloomy landscape made it easy for me to notice a bonus in the August 1998 issue: A smaller magazine within the larger magazine (Magazineception!!) dedicated to an upcoming RPG series called Pokémon. The mini-mag was presented as a travel document you might take with you while on vacation to a foreign land. It got in-depth about Pokémon, their habits, and the best ways to catch them. It preemptively answered questions about Pokémon types and the ultimate challenge of "Catching 'em All."

"Pokémon Power" was just one questing root that preceded a deluge of Pokémon media, which itself preceded the September 28 release of *Pokémon Red* and *Pokémon Blue* for the Game Boy. I remember initially thinking that it was weird to see a Game Boy game make waves. The little brick was hanging in there but the glory days of *Tetris* were long behind it. That said, I still only needed to read half of that premiere issue of *Pokémon Power* to realize "Holy shit. This Pokémon thing is going to be *huge*."

Pokémon screenshots showed a turn-based RPG with an overworld that barely contained more detail than *Dragon Warrior* for the NES — a game I loved, but also a game that was downright archaic in 1998. That was the compromise for Game Freak pouring all of Pokémon's secret design sauce into making the titular Pokémon as charming as possible. Not an easy thing to do when your canvas is the Game Boy's cabbage-coloured screen, but Game Freak made it happen. And whenever *Pokémon*'s now-iconic monster sprites fell short of sparking kids' imaginations, the localized Pokémon anime from production company 4Kids filled the gaps with monsters that ran and roared and flung elemental attacks at each other. Pokémon wasn't simply huge. It was a phenomenon unlike any I'd seen blossom until then, or since.

I was in my late teens by the time the anime hit western TV with nuclear force, so I felt a bit too old for it. I never touched Pokémon cards because collecting those cards was the pastime of the criminally insane, as it continues to be. But as a diehard fan of RPGs, I gobbled *Pokémon Red* right up. I'd chosen my starter (Charmander) before the game came west. *Pokémon Red*'s simple battle commands and UI combined with its monster menagerie to construct an ingenious debut for a property that is now recognized on every corner of the Earth. Kids probably get into the Pokémon anime or other merchandise long before they're even capable of gumming on a Game Boy. It's funny to look back and realize I took the humblest door into the Pokémon phenomenon.The actual Pokémon games are still my biggest emotional investment in the multi-tentacled franchise to this day.

(I will admit I do have some Pokémon merch, including some of the first toys and figures to come west. I have a Pikachu toy that says its own name when you press the connectors on its yellow butt. When I first showed it off to a friend, Pikachu was still such an unknown that my friend wanted to know why I had a toy that said "Kick a Jew.")

Adults who forgot they were once into weird ironic shit like pet rocks were baffled at Pokémon's popularity. Anyone who loved adventure stories growing up shouldn't have a hard time understanding why Pokémon continues to enthrall kids. It's a tale about throwing off school, work, and other responsibilities to go on a cross-country coming-of-age quest. No parents. No homework. No bullies barring occasional run-ins with a rival who's dumb enough to have a Raticate in his party, so who cares what he thinks? (No shade Raticate, I heart you.) And, best of all, you take this journey alongside a hand-picked menagerie of pets that understand English perfectly and never poop on the floor at midnight.

I got through to some folks, but plenty couldn't shake the scales from their eyes. "Children today can remember the names of 151 of these 'Pokémon', but they can't remember the names of our Presidents!" the 6 o'clock news cried out. Who even condemns kids for not knowing the Presidents' names? Do *adults* know them?

Pokémon came of age around the same time AOL began mailing discs containing "free internet access!" (not actually free) to homes all over the United States. Kids started using the internet from home and quickly bonded to the budding Pokémon online community. They found a place amongst a new generation of fan creators that wrote tomes of Pokémon fanfiction and drew sheafs of Pokémon fanart. For many amateur creators Pokémon's online community was the genesis of their creative expression. And for moms and dads, it was the genesis for epic tug-of-war matches over the phone line. It was the '90s greatest struggle. Telephone or modem: There can be only one [running at a time].

I'd long since established my claim on Mega Man's online community by that point and Pokémon didn't interest me enough to get deep into another fandom. Yet I still felt strong enough about Pokémon to feature it in a small piece of writing I made years later, some time after a potential career choice drifted out of my reach.

I've always loved animals. When I was a toddler my grandparents' German shepherds trailed me like tamed direwolves. As a kid I'd follow animals around, desperate to find a way to talk to them. I worked in the field for several years as an assistant dog/cat groomer, and if you think you don't need epic cross-species communication abilities to coax a 150-pound mastiff into a bathtub, man, have I got news for you.

Part of growing up and growing old is craning your neck backwards and thinking "Crap, did I miss my exit?" as you ride the Highway of Life. I'm not at all dissatisfied with how my life turned out other than being dirt-poor through most of it. But sometimes I feel like there was a point in my life when I was supposed to go to college for Communications, get a proper job, and invent an English-to-Dolphinese translator or something. My chronic pain issues and lack of higher education closed the door on *that* canon event a while ago, which is why you're all stuck with me here in Videoland.

But it's not so bad. Playing Pokémon across the decades has made me appreciate how much Game Freak loves nerding out about animal taxonomy and zoology in general. 2016's *Pokémon Sun* and *Pokémon Moon* for the Nintendo 3DS still ranks as my favourite Pokémon game because Game Freak put so much thought into the Alola region's environment. Alola is a Hawaii analogue, and its wild Pokémon reflect real life examples of Hawaiian animals affected by colonization. Sugarcane was a valuable commodity grown on the Big Island through the 19th century, but the rats who arrived on the ships of the colonizers developed a taste for the sweet sticks. The non-native mongoose was released in Hawaii *en masse* to control the sugar-drunk rodents. There was just one problem: Rats are active at night, whereas mongooses hunt during the day. The mongooses largely ignored the rats, but they developed an unfortunate appetite for the island's many ground-nesting birds. Native Hawaiian species are literal sitting ducks while the descendents of these voracious hunters pick them off.

Pokémon Sun and *Moon* has a parallel instance of the mongoose's failed introduction to Hawaii. The Normal-type Pokémon Yungoos resembles the real-world mongoose, albeit with a permanent and ferocious scowl that'd be more at home on a great white shark. According to the PokéDex, Yongoos was "imported" to Alola from another region after the Rattatas who hitched rides on cargo ships bred out of control. The Rattatas adapted to the Yongoos threat by changing their type from Normal to Dark/Normal. In other words, the Rattatas evolved to become a nocturnal species while the Yongooses continued to live in the daylight.

That's so *cool.* At least I think so. Pokémon designs are given much more thought than people think at first glance. Even when a Pokémon is a conglomerate of weird artistic choices, there's a reason why they look stupid and it's usually related to their survival. Take Sandygast, an actual sandpile Pokémon that was introduced in, again, *Pokémon Sun* and *Moon.* Sandygast is one of those Pokémon everyone hated when it was first introduced, and they cited it as example #593047 of Game Freak "running out of ideas." But when you read the Ghost/ Ground-type's PokéDex entry, you learn amazing trivia like how Sandygast makes sand traps to trap wayward Pokémon and drain their life force. The shovel on top of its head coaxes children to add sand to its mobile pile until it gets bigger and bigger. In time, it evolves into Palossand, a sentient sand castle that can ensnare large prey, drain them of vitality at its leisure, then fire the victim's bones at threats. Man.

Sandygast and Palossand are the opposite of braindead Pokémon designs. They're the careful work of a studio that understands sometimes nature is cool and nice, and sometimes it's weird and ugly. All things, people and Pokémon alike, need to do what they can to survive.

Pokémon biology is weird and impossible, and the Pokémon themselves sometimes interact in wonderful ways. I started to appreciate Pokémon's "science" around the same time the series started feeding me crazy shit about pink cows hatching out of eggs. I started asking myself unanswerable questions about how Pokémon's reproductive organs work, which in turn got me thinking about a veterinarian's role in the Pokémon world. Sure, sick or injured Pokémon could get fixed right up at the Pokémon Centre, but those aren't on every corner. What happens to Pokémon working on farms and the like?

My beloved 1UP.com was emitting death rattles by 2012. One of its last big projects was "Science Week," a series of features that made tongue-in-cheek "studies" about the wonky science that drives many games. I immediately knew I wanted to write something about Pokémon's bizarre bods, but I wasn't sure how to present my fake report.

This was also around the same time I got deep into *If Only They Could Talk* and other books about the adventures of James Herriot, a country vet who practised in Yorkshire for over 50 years starting in 1940. Herriot's books get elbow-deep into topics like low-tech solutions for a prolapsed cow uterus. (Sugar, by the way.) Much of Herriot's early experiences involved visiting farms at three in the freezing a.m. to fix up cows, sheep, and horses. I thought to myself, "A lot of this can be applied to the Pokémon world."

I also recognized my rapidly-growing idea had the potential to get a little crazy, so I made my main character an utter Stranger in a Strange Land — a country veterinarian who somehow finds herself in the world of Pokémon. And thus my first paid-for fanfiction was born. In "Welcome to Kanto Region, Doctor" a nameless veterinarian who's new to Kanto becomes irritated with a young client named Blue ("You don't look depressed") whose Miltank is having trouble laying her egg. The baffled vet thinks someone's having a laugh at her expense. Blue is just irritated that this "expert" doesn't know that pink cows lay eggs. He also complains that he's probably in for a scolding by his Grandfather who thinks the solution to a Pokemon's ills is to believe in the power of friendship.

The final product, "Welcome to Kanto Region, Doctor," was born. It's short, and unlike some of my other works, it doesn't embarrass me beyond belief because its core idea is solid. I think my inborn curiosity about animals and the satisfaction of documenting them means I'll be a Pokémon fan for life. And I'll be first in line when someone inevitably engineers them into living beings. I'm dying to sink my fingers into an Arcanine's flowing mane as we gallop across Kanto like Aslan carrying Susan and Lucy across Narnia.

CHAPTER 8

Erotic Writing Lessons Learned from Undertale's Bone Zone

"I'm not ready for this to end. I'm not ready for you to leave. I'm not ready to say goodbye to someone like you again..." - Asriel, *Undertale*

On March 30, 2016, a Twitter user calling themselves "Vaping Toriel" ("g0atm0m") tweeted, "No, I am NOT the Toriel cosplayer that gave that dude a blowjob and stole his wallet. I'm married and i have no idea where dragoncon even is."

The tweet is still there, accompanied by a profile picture of a cosplayer dressed as a smock-wearing anthropomorphic goat. The goat is vaping with the serene expression of a barnyard animal that knows it's innocent of exploiting people's new, weird kinks while pilfering their wallets. But that means a rogue goat might still be out there somewhere, administering oral delights to people and nicking their coinage at the most opportune moment.

Vaping Toriel's tweet, not to mention their very schtick, would have been dismissed as gibberish even a day before September 15, 2015. But we were living in a post-*Undertale* world by March 2016, and every gamer had thoroughly lost their minds by then.

I participated in the fervor, obviously. I thought, and still think, *Undertale* is gaming's best-told story.

Undertale is an RPG by Toby Fox, a game developer and musician from New Hampshire. Fox got his start as a developer by doing fan hacks of *Earthbound*, the much-beloved SNES RPG that got a big jolt in popularity thanks to endless gong-banging from a dedicated fanbase at Starmen.net. Fox was also involved in the baffling digital comic series *Homestuck* by Andrew Hussie, to which he contributed reams of music that narrate the adventures of its popular "Troll" characters. One of Fox's works for *Homestuck* is "The Baby is You," a song about one Troll character giving birth to another. Years later, "The Baby is You" was reworked into the Battle Tower theme for *Pokémon Sword* and *Pokémon Shield*. That's right, by November 2019, Toby Fox had so thoroughly upended the RPG space that he was invited to compose official music for Pokémon.

Every once in a great while, an RPG breaks away from the fandom and charms outsiders into loving the genre. *Final Fantasy VII* is a good example, especially in the west. But *Final Fantasy VII* arguably drew westerners in with Sony-funded commercials that stitched together its pre-rendered cutscenes. The ads spoiled us on Aerith's death in between episodes of Johnny Bravo, but we were too pumped to care. I'll hazard a guess that a whole lot of *Final Fantasy VII* buyers thought the entire game would be cinematic non-stop action, like the ads implied. I can't imagine everyone who picked up Cloud's adventure was happy to find themselves plodding through menus and reading reams of text. Still, plenty of players found good reasons to stick around even after the shine of the cinematic cutscenes had worn off. They became invested in the complex story, its iconic cast of characters, and its mechanics.

Undertale doesn't have the visual pull of Square Enix's best cinemas. It's not a *bad* looking game, but one glance tells you its pedigree as an independent RPG put together with GameMaker's drag-and-drop process. Its overworld graphics aren't much fancier than what you'll find in a 16-bit RPG circa the early '90s. Animated monster sprites take over the screen when the gameplay shifts to an encounter with potential hostiles, but these sprites are likewise plain-looking at first glance.

But by your third journey down *Undertale*'s tortuous story paths, you will know every single monster's name. You will be familiarized with the charm that *Undertale* artist Temmie Chang baked into every monster. You will know every single Froggit, every single Snowdrake, every single Shyren. And though your mother's caked blood dulls your knife, you sink its blade into them one after another. After another. Until the forests and fields are as silent as Death's shroud, and the friendly monsters populating the Underworld's towns burrow deep for safety. Until you've smashed every guardian and would-be hero who'd stop your reunion with the inner darkness you've kept stifled for so, so long.

You might also become the saviour of monsterkind, a pure-hearted messiah who soothes a troubled goat boy's soul and restores peace between monsters and humans. It depends which order you're playing the story in. Protip: You're not supposed to slaughter *Undertale*'s monsters when you first meet them, but no one's really going to stop you. Wait, scratch that. Two characters *will* try very, *very* hard to stop you if you go down the crimson trail of *Undertale*'s infamous genocide route. Prepare thy kitchen knife.

Undertale is the "Alice in Wonderland" of RPGs. The rules that govern the dance of the universe don't necessarily apply to Toby Fox's game. Its characters don't just push the fourth wall — they draw a dong on it and kick it down like cheap drywall. Though you travel through the game as a blank-faced child named Frisk, it's not long before some of *Undertale*'s characters begin talking to *you* directly. You, with the game installed on your PC. You, the one who's ultimately pushing the buttons that choose the fate of every monster you meet on your journey, innocent or otherwise.

Upending game mechanics and forcing players to look at themselves and their choices was a popular design choice long before *Undertale* existed. *Ultima: Quest of the Avatar* by genius astronaut/game developer Richard Garriott still does a good job of testing players' morals despite being an Apple][RPG from 1985. And Toby Fox makes no secret of the fact *Undertale* owes a chunk of its existence to an obscure PlayStation RPG that turns a critical eye towards fans of the genre.

1997's *Moon: Remix RPG Adventure* for the PlayStation is an RPG where you, a non-playable character ("NPC"), tries to clean up after a hero who's wreaking havoc on his journey to kill the ultimate evil. *Moon* was designed in part by Kenichi Nishi, a former designer at SquareSoft who knows a thing or two about darkly humourous RPG tropes. Yes, we all put on our shining armour and take an oath to slay some great demon, only to immediately burst into the King's bedroom and rummage around in his nightstand for goodies. Yes, we all put on a green tunic and start flinging people's pottery everywhere, as if on instinct. We gladly steal citizens' half-smoked "medical herbs" and couch cushion change. (As measured in zenny, gil, or gold pieces.) *Moon*'s message is as subtle as a Mack Truck to the face, but it's not wrong: We just feel compelled to act like dicks when we step into NPCs' houses. Heck, we feel like we're *entitled* to be dicks. If an RPG hands me boxes and barrels that can't be destroyed or searched through, I get crabby. I get crabby if I can't steal some NPC's life savings of 20 gold pieces stuffed in a kitchen drawer! Like, damn! What is wrong with me?

On November 17, 2017, Toby Fox tweeted confirmation that *Moon*'s bizarro take on RPG cliches directly inspired *Undertale*'s deep examination of players' unquestioned habits. *Moon* and Nishi deserve great respect, but *Moon*'s core examination of player behaviours in RPGs struck me as a little preachy when I played its first official translation in August 2020. *Moon*'s concept is still fascinating, and *Undertale* successfully builds tiers upon it by weaving story paths populated by charming monsters you befriend and maybe kill as you uproot the underground realm's awful secrets.To put it another way, I didn't do myself or *Moon* any favours by playing *Undertale* first.

Like *Moon,* one of *Undertale*'s core messages is to be kind and understanding even when you're a stranger in a strange land. You and Frisk "win" if you manage to liberate monsterkind from their underground imprisonment and bring the two races together again without ever lifting your knife. That's the "True Pacifist" route, which leads to *Undertale*'s canon ending.

If you go into *Undertale* blind, you will probably kill at least one monster in self-defence. This puts you on one of several "Neutral" routes and subsequent ending scenarios. Neutral endings can range from an amicable departure from monsterland to dark, eerie finales that conclude with a black screen and the sound of howling wind.

Once you're well-acquainted with *Undertale*'s cast, you're given the option to do a terrible and interesting thing. You can turn Frisk into a killer as soon as they fall down into the underworld. Frisk has access to a knife early in *Undertale*'s narrative. Pacifists don't touch the weapon. The Frisk of *Undertale*'s "Genocide Route," however, is the cold stone opposite of a pacifist. Knife ever-unsheathed, they pounce on every monster that crosses them — including Toriel, the motherly goat who allegedly likes vaping. Toriel is your first roadblock in each *Undertale* story path. She tries to stop Frisk from leaving her care, warning them that death awaits on the outside.

Your method of getting around Toriel is a major path marker in *Undertale*. If you're a pacifist, you can have Frisk withstand her fire magic, and then appeal to her matronly soul by refusing to lift a finger in self-defence. If you're a genocidal maniac, you can order Frisk to use their knife, which they gladly will. Over and over. And as Toriel's fading eyes fill with the horror of what she's inadvertently let loose on the monsters of the underworld, Frisk steps over her and begins a gory campaign of hateful vengeance that's impossible to understand until dark explanations gradually unfurl.

When you start weaving the story strands between *Undertale*'s three main story pillars, you come to learn Frisk's black pilgrimage echoes the behaviour of another child who fell into monster country a long time ago. That wide-eyed, waxen-faced child was named Chara, and they left indelible black marks on the kindly monsters who adopted them — including Toriel, who then reigned Queen of monsterkind alongside King Asgore Dreemur, a tremendous slab of cape-wearing bull meat with a soft-boiled heart.

Chara's penchant for violent mischief surfaced again and again until one last "game" caused their death. Humans initially believed Chara was killed by their adoptive brother and best friend, the monster prince named Asriel Dreemur. The event destroyed the truce between humans and monsters, the latter of whom were sealed in their underworld kingdom under Mount Ebott.

When Frisk falls down into the underworld some years later, Chara's prank and subsequent death has shattered the Dreemur royal family, and the monster population is fragmented. King Asgore is driven to bring his people back to the surface, though his method of doing so is grisly and disturbing. Toriel, now separated from Asgore, keeps vigil in the ruins and takes care of the occasional human child who climbs Mount Ebott and falls into monster land. But the children always detach from Toriel's care and leave the ruins to enter the underworld proper, where they invariably die. Asgore kills each child himself, harvesting their powerful young souls for the energy he needs to breach the barrier that keeps his people sealed away. Toriel laments she hasn't been able to save a single child, but she knows she must let Frisk slip from her to journey through her broken kingdom, confront Asgore, and return home. And journey Frisk shall, whether lovingly or violently.

As is wont to happen with RPGs, *Undertale*'s simple quest to get back home gradually becomes more complicated. The monster kingdom has dark secrets that twist far beneath its bedrock, and Frisk is pulled into untangling some of these story threads as they travel towards Asgore. They learn how Chara, the previous fallen child, was a manipulator who coerced the monster prince Asriel into playing the "prank" that led to their death and ignited the war between humans and monsters.

But there are darker secrets still, ghosts and monstrosities that lurk in a haunting underground medical facility called the True Lab. These abominations were born of good-intentioned experiments to give monsters a chance against humans, but good intentions don't change the fact these specimens resemble primordial slime more than living beings. The road to Hell isn't paved with rainbow gumdrops.

Chara. Asriel. Asgore. The War. The True Lab and its groaning crop of half-monsters. Everything connects, as Frisk learns when they complete the True Pacifist ending. Dragging a light on the truth behind the experiments and the real catalyst behind the monster-human war doesn't reveal a pretty scene, but once it's out in the air, Frisk is able to bring the monster-human war to a bloodless end. *Undertale* taught me there's surprising satisfaction to finishing an epic quest without peeling a single hit point off a monster. I very much enjoyed the challenge. No matter how much crazy robot David Bowie impersonator Mettaton deserved a punch in the face for his distracting limb-flailing antics.

But…

Undertale's True Pacifist ties up a lot of story threads, save for a couple that dangle in the shadows and dare you to pull them. If you walk away from *Undertale* at this point, you can sleep soundly knowing the monsters integrated into human society and Frisk was never again without family and friends. That might not be enough, however, depending on the kind of person you are. You might find yourself wondering about Chara, the first fallen child. Who were they? What hurt them badly enough that they'd mistreat the family that adopted them? And what if Flowey, the self-proclaimed puppeteer of *Undertale*'s story, isn't as hard as he tries to be? What if he's just a cold, flower-shaped vessel born of Asriel Dreemur's ashes? A living being that's bereft of a soul and therefore susceptible to being led around like a goat on a rope?

Undertale's Genocide Route ties up those dangling threads, but travelling down that road comes at the hefty cost of your soul. I couldn't finish my massacre of *Undertale*'s citizens; the emotional toll made moving through the plot feel like walking on Legos. Turning on the underworld's motley monsters is a betrayal. When you act with kindness, the monsters gradually act in turn. And when they open up to you, you're treated to some of the funniest, most heartfelt writing dished out by an RPG. You convince the kingdom's sworn protector, Undyne the Undying, to lay down her spear and cook with you. You go on a date with Papyrus, a skeleton whose huge heart compensates for his empty braincase. You learn about the prophecy of hope that every monster clings to as they wait for the barrier to fall. And finally, you restore the hollow soul of Asriel Dreemur, the lonely goat prince who just wanted his friend back.

Toby Fox does a hell of a thing by introducing us to our new family before handing us a knife and suggesting we split open their guts to see absolutely everything *Undertale* has to offer. Do you *have* to go on a killing spree? Of course not; that's why God invented YouTube. Watching someone else play through *Undertale*'s Genocide Route isn't a whole lot easier, but there are some important revelations on the red path. Once you start killing, *Undertale*'s story structure starts wobbling. The narrative about Asgore, the barrier, and the monsters' freedom quickly dissolves as your kill count gets higher. You become the obvious embodiment of Chara. And then you simply become something that other characters can only identify as inhuman.

Playing through *Undertale*'s Genocide Route is also the only way to access its superboss fights. When it becomes obvious you're a psychopath, two of the monsters' best warriors move to stop you, like white blood cells deployed to purge a dangerous new virus. First is Undyne the Undying, who proves to be a good cooking partner if she likes you, and a bladed nightmare if she doesn't. She immediately recognizes you as a threat to monsters, to humans, to existence itself, and unlike the small fry you've diced up until this point, she's not easily killed. Undyne is a deadly lancer who's made even deadlier when the land itself lends her the collective hope and determination of the monsters she's protecting from your violence. Undyne literally has the power of God and anime on her side.

Some *Undertale* fans describe Undyne as a hero not only because she stands up to you, but also because the fight against her is difficult enough to push most people off the Genocide Path. If your bruised conscience can't deter you from slaughtering monsters, Undyne's relentless attacks combined with her cheetah-grade speed will at least slow you down. Like all of *Undertale*'s fights, the battle against Undyne interlaces traditional RPG menus with action sequences that resemble bite-sized "bullet hell" experiences. Bullet hells are a sub-genre of shoot-em-up games where enemy projectiles fill the entire screen, often in hypnotically beautiful patterns that blossom like lethal flowers. Your own craft, which can range from a spaceship to a dragon to an anime girl depending on the game you're playing, typically has a tiny hitbox. Bullet hell games are about dancing within a pixel's breadth of death while counterattacking, and that's what *Undertale*'s battle against Undyne is all about.

Your craft in *Undertale*'s bullet hell interludes is represented by a tiny heart — the physical manifestation of your rotten, stinking soul. You must shield yourself against Undyne's rain of spears, then dodge more spears that poke up from the bottom of the battlefield. You also have to contend with Undyne's penchant for limiting your movement by messing with the size and gravitational pull of the arena. But if you're determined to ruin every monster kid's favourite hero, you'll get your chance to counterattack. Dodge, then dive in. Like a snake.

Playing *Undertale*'s Genocide Route is like entering the game through the backstage area. It's the only path that lets you get familiar with *Undertale*'s most cherished character: Sans, a short slipper-wearing skeleton with a dad gut. Some of *Undertale*'s funniest writing comes from Sans, whose perpetual grin and love for jokes will put you at ease — if he likes you. Once Sans recognizes you as a threat to the monster kingdom, it only takes a few terse words to turn that grin into a grimace of intent. If you don't chill out, he will intervene. And if Sans needs to step in, you are, as the famous quote goes, "Gonna have a bad time."

Sans is *Undertale*'s Gandalf. He knows what's going on everywhere, all the time. He can warp time and space, and he can access fearfully powerful attacks when necessary. And, like Gandalf, Sans loves to take it easy with the mere mortals of the world. You'll find him in places like cafes and restaurants, and behind impromptu booths selling hot dogs. (And a hot cat, if you patronize him enough.) If you play *Undertale* with honest intent, Sans becomes your most powerful ally and friend. But if you arrive in the underground bearing Chara's essence, Sans makes it clear that if you start anything, he will end it.

If you goad Sans into bringing everything to bear — a necessity if you want to see your massacre to its bitter, black end — he will drop his big buddy skeleton act and engage you in a fight like you've never had in an RPG. Undyne is a kindergartner with a stick compared to Sans' reality-tearing onslaught. It's nearly indescribable: You need to personally witness first-hand as Sans disassembles reality and exploits long-lived RPG genre tropes in his determination to save monsterkind and the world itself against you and the festering shadow of Chara that stretches behind your feet.

If you cannot defeat Sans, and there is an *excellent* chance you won't, you can try again. And again. As many times as it takes. In fact, your only hope is to memorize Sans' patterns and dodge like hell while waiting for the chance to strike. He has one hit point, which technically makes him one of the weakest monsters in the game. Problem is, Sans is a veteran dimension-hopper who's harder to hit than a greased-up pygmy mouse. Good luck landing that killing blow.

Sans also *knows* that you're memorizing his patterns in these repeat battles, and he will absolutely play dirty and trip you up. For example, Sans gives a small speech every time you engage him. ("On days like these, kids like you…should be burning in hell.") Lots of RPG super-bosses will exchange words with you before attacking, but they won't pounce until they're finished with their piece. Sans, however, will not hesitate to randomly send you flying before he's done talking. Hey! That's not fair! Sure isn't! But if you're that serious about slicing away Sans' sole hit point, you'd better get used to low blows. And you deserve every single whack to the nuts, literal, metaphorical, or otherwise.

It's actually impossible to take down Sans in a fair fight, but the magical space skeleton has one weakness: He's a sleepy boy. Probably a result of vaping too much magic cabbage with Toriel. Or maybe hand-to-knife combat with a sweater-wearing incarnation of Beezlebub is just that exhausting. Either way, Sans makes a fatal mistake by dozing off after using the last of his strength to bind you in limbo. The small square battlefield you two just raged over and across might restrain you, but it's not anchored in place. If you move slowly and carefully, you just might be able to drag your prison down to the unguarded "Fight" button…and take care of that pesky single hit point that stands between you and utter destruction of the world. But when everything is dark and silent, Chara murders you as well. Darkness is voracious, and once the light's gone out, it can only consume itself. That's the price for digging up every last scrap of *Undertale*'s story. Is that information worth the permanent stain on your sole save file? Was it worth the heartbreak of turning your new buddies into monster confetti? How about all the time you sank into memorizing Undyne and Sans' attack patterns so you could break your fingers weaving and dodging their hail of attacks?

Lest you think I'm trying to shame you for finishing *Undertale* to its bitter end, that's not the case. If Toby Fox hadn't wanted you to find this dark path, he wouldn't have presented it as a possibility. When an *Undertale* player takes Frisk down to Murder Town, it's proof of *Undertale*'s power as a story-telling device. Again, games had already been coming up with ways to upend its own narrative by that point, but it was rare for story and gameplay to touch on such an intimate level. *Undertale* is a game that acknowledges it's a game. Its story isn't a script that moves its characters from battle to battle like a theatre production. Its narrative is entwined in the game's mechanics, and even its code.

If you haven't played *Undertale,* I recommend getting it on the PC, the platform it was originally built for. It plays some pretty haunting tricks with save files, game "crashes," and other shenanigans that are chilling if you have a deep-seated fear of technology yanking control from humanity's hands. Maybe I'm just a little scaredy-baby, but I find something inherently creepy about the sounds and sights of '80s–'90s technology breaking down. Back in the day, computers didn't give us twee "Oh no!" messages when they encountered a problem. They just shit themselves and left behind frozen screens, blaring static, or angry buzzing. By 1992, my NES had a 50–50 chance of interrupting my *Super Mario Bros. 3* playthrough with a digital scream that froze Mario as a mishmash of red pixels and brown numbers. That's a lot to live with, and I'm from the generation that endured the television going "*eeeeeeeeeeee*" at us during commercial breaks for "She-Ra" because, you know, someone might hit Da Button that ignites thermonuclear war. Don't worry, though. This is only a test.

I'm weirdly glad Toby Fox managed to bottle up that specific fear and mix it into *Undertale*'s story delivery. This is one of those situations where you think to yourself, "I must be the only doofus who has this fear," but given how skillfully Fox delivered *Undertale*'s "sentient game" moments, I'm clearly not.

I believe *Undertale* is, and will remain, the quintessential example of story and gameplay meshing into a true player-driven experience. It's enduring proof that every inch of a video game, right down to its code, can deliver a storytelling experience that differs from movies and books in unique, important ways. *Undertale* changed RPGs forever, and — oh, wait. Hold on. We can't close off this celebration without acknowledging the naked skeleton in the room. We need to talk about how and why *Undertale*'s characters, especially Sans, took erotic fanfic tropes to levels previously unimagined. And we need to somehow keep it PG-13.

As a dusty Xillenial, it was enlightening to watch Millennials unravel over *Undertale* and pen lurid fantasies about a skeleton named after a font nobody likes. It was definitely a personal learning experience about how people use fanfiction to explore "weird" sexual desires as SansBlueBoner4577 because dear God their parents can *never* know.

I started writing and publishing [*cough*] Mega Man stories in 1995. Women have long played a huge role in cultivating and tending the modern fanfiction scene, but Mega Man's fanfiction authors at the time were overwhelmingly male. With exceptions, of course: Shout out to writer/artist Mandi Paugh, whose Mega Man/Captain N: The Game Master crossover fanfictions are still archived on The Mega Man Home Page. But Paugh's charming work is intentionally family friendly, and I was *too cool* for that in 1995. The stories I read were usually violent, with a lot of instances of series protagonists X and Zero bashing the crap out of each other. The most recent Mega Man game release in those very early days of online fandom, *Mega Man X3,* ended with a prophecy stating X would have to kill Zero, so of course everyone went bananas and typed words to fill probability's void.

I wouldn't call the fanfic I grew up with "chaste," but its young authors didn't spend a lot of time writing mushy scenes. We were barely old enough to know how human sex worked, and it took a little time for us to get comfortable talking about robots banging and sliding across the floor like your mother's old washing machine and dryer. The shyness passed and eager conversation eventually began, but by then I couldn't join in because I was too busy with stupid dumb-dumb adult things like working and paying rent. You cannot pay your landlord with fanfiction of *Monopoly*'s Rich Uncle Pennybags getting stomped by the proletariat. I have tried.

Undertale fans, unlike my earliest fanfic-writing posse, didn't hesitate to get weird about falling in love with its myriad monsters and robots. I admit I was surprised at how quickly and thoroughly the fanbase was for Sans. I'm no babe in the woods — I understand fantasy and escapism, especially sex-related fantasy and escapism, has always been a driving force for fanfiction. It's one of the medium's biggest *raisons d'etre.* Heck, I was desensitised to the internet's wanton monster lust long before *Undertale*'s release. I remember scrolling through Tumblr in its glory years and seeing pictures of things like naked, greased-up werewolves fighting over a piece of pizza while searching for Phoenix Wright fanart. And one day I realized I no longer batted an eye at most titillating monster fanart. It's not as if I'd say "no" to a werewolf, it's just that admitting as much is as vanilla as declaring you're a fan of drug store pulp novels. These days, nobody is a freak just because they want to boff a ghost or a Dracula.

But Sans? Sans is a skeleton.

How…does a skeleton?...

To steal and mangle a quote from the great Dr. Ian Malcom, "fandom, uh, finds a way." I'm not going to get into any lurid details, but let's just say Sans' schleppy jacket and shorts potentially cover up some non-bony anatomy. But does flesh really matter when you're with an awakened being who can summon literally anything from the void? Literally…anything?

Sans' Swiss army anatomy is still a fertile [*COUGH*] outlet for fanfic writers who are exploring their own fantasies and their own sexual identities. Especially gay, trans, and otherwise queer folks who find Sans shape-shifting compelling. If *Undertale* has one additional message to deliver, it's that the bar that society uses to measure what's "normal" wobbles a lot.

Another secret to *Undertale*'s sauce is how it doesn't waste a single storytelling component. Every monster, every lonely locale, every piece of snail pie (thank you for referencing my beloved *Illusion of Gaia*, Fox), and every letter of text works equally hard to guide you through an unforgettable adventure.

The experience is wrapped up in what is without exaggeration one of the best video game soundtracks in gaming history. As talented as Toby Fox is as a game developer, he's ten times more talented as a music composer. No ordinary schmuck with a keyboard goes from tinkering with SNES music for fan projects to composing music for Pokémon games.

Maybe we were unravelled by *Undertale*'s soundtrack alone, even if we're not consciously aware of it. Have you ever been to a concert with a bunch of nerds? If the atmosphere calls for it, introverts turn feral when music goes hard. Especially Sonic fans. I went to a Sonic the Hedgehog anniversary concert once, and the whole event could have been powered by the frantic energy crackling in the air. Sonic fans are capable of tapping into a vein of energy I can't see. I guess that's the benefit of having Super Sonic as your Lord and Saviour.

Undertale plunked into the middle of the video game scene almost ten years ago, and its ripples of influence are still bobbing through the fanfic community. I hope it continues to be a rich playground for new writers. New writers, old farts, veterans, novices — everyone can learn something from *Undertale* and its trophy skeleton, Sans. Maybe more than you want to know.

CHAPTER 9

Life, the Universe, and Anime Tropes

"Ours is not a kind world, but it is beautiful. Always." - Alphinaud Leveilleur, *Final Fantasy XIV: Endwalker*

My parents were religious whenever my grandparents looked their way, so I suppose I grew up with more Orthodox Jewish-learning than the average Canadian rascal. I even attended Hebrew school on alternating weeknights and Sundays. But my parents also turned on WWF's Maple Leaf Wrestling for us when we got home from synagogue and otherwise used electronics that are traditionally forbidden on the Day of Rest in Orthodox Judaism. So I hope it's not too much of a shock for anyone when I admit it was a pair of video games and not religion, philosophy, or education that made me rethink life, the universe, and everything.

Well, not at first. Please don't take this as a sign my philosophical outlook on the world is shaped exclusively by games. I strongly believe it's beneficial to forge a life path using as many outlets available to you as possible, including digital, analogue, and hands-on. Then you can die enlightened but hungry because you didn't spend that time looking for a decent job. Life is beautiful.

There's still no point in denying that a video game story might open your mind if you're subjected to it during a certain time in your life — e.g. when you're somewhere between 14 and 19 years old and you think you're hot shit even as you latch onto story cliches that barely challenge Japanese schoolchildren. Cliches like sneering villains reminding heroes that light can't exist without darkness. Cliches like heroes suffering existential crises as they come to terms with the dark impulses within themselves. Cliches like literal forces of Nature and the Universe visiting humankind and demanding to know what, if anything, makes humans worthy stewards of Earth.

And you know something? Those are some pretty bad-ass cliches. If we've learned anything during our time together, I hope I've made it clear that good story delivery counts for more than "bringing something new to the table."

Final Fantasy XIV's 2019 expansion, *Shadowbringers*, finally broke the Final Fantasy fans who swore they'd never play an online Final Fantasy game, myself included. At the climax of the story, which is still one of the best written for a game, you confront the immortal Emet-Selch, a man-god whose long, *long* life has him despairing at the thought of mortals inheriting the planet from his near-extinct race. "Look at me!" Emet-Selch snarls at you in the depths of the illusory city he conjured to ease his millenia of loneliness. "I have lived a thousand, *thousand* of your lives! I have broken bread with you, fought with you, grown ill, grown old! Sired children and yes, welcomed death's sweet embrace. For eons have I measured your worth and found you wanting! Too weak and feeble-minded to serve as stewards of any star!"

Emet-Selch's rant, born from equal parts spite and heartbreak, is delivered with perfect venom by voice actor Rene Zagger. Taken in the context of *Shadowbringers'* story, it's one of the most poignant climaxes a game has delivered to date. That's despite the fact Emet-Selch is just barking out the same question that pops up in Japanese media from the cutest anime to the most serious of manga, games, and novels: What have we humans done to prove we deserve to exist? What would happen if a space alien or a sentient AI or a sad but extremely powerful man held a world-destroying weapon to humanity's collective face and said "Prove your species has been a net gain for the planet?" We'd better start doing some fancy talking.

It's unlikely some outside force will ever land on Earth and challenge us to justify our existence. It's just a nice bit of philosophical gristle that even a kid can chew on for a lifetime. If, however, that revelation smacks into you when you're an anime-obsessed teen, the impact is like a comet. For '80s and '90s kids in particular, it was a marked difference from the flaccid moral messages we got from cartoons like *G.I. Joe.* (To be totally fair to the '90s, it's not like we even managed to digest the pablum. There are actual villains from *James Bond Jr.* in the Supreme Court right now.)

Most Christian kids in North America also grow up with an inflexible doctrine about the afterlife: There's Good, and there's Evil. There's a Heaven where God lives, there's a Hell where Satan lives, and maybe there's a Limbo or a Purgatory. Christians have gone to war over the specifics, e.g. what *exactly* a soul needs to do if they want to spend an eternity in the Glory of the Lord instead of an eternity under Satan's left ass cheek, but that's the gist of it.

But Christianity kind of lost its shine in Japan after the torture and crucifixtion of the 26 Martyrs in 1597, so missionaries chilled and minded their own business for a long while. Christianity is practised in modern Japan, but according to (the online) *Encyclopedia Britannica*, Japanese citizens overwhelmingly follow Buddhism, Shintoism, or a mix of the two. I'm not going to pretend I'm a scholar on Shōwa- and Heisei-era Japanese religion and culture, but I always figured the deep questions we see in its anime, games, and other media are owed to the country's Buddhist and nature-worshipping roots. Even the most generic sentai villain will eventually ask its young audience to give it one good reason why humanity's existence matters in a cold, infinite universe. You're never too young for your first existential crisis.

An interesting thing a lot of people don't know about Judaism is that it doesn't evangelize about the afterlife. The general consensus amongst secular Jews and scholars alike is that there's no way to prove what happens when we die, therefore it's probably better to concentrate on living instead. It was nice to grow up without nightmares about going to Hell or being left behind in the Rapture, but it also meant I didn't think about the spiritual side of my faith when I was young. Our prayers were in Hebrew, which I didn't understand, and when my family went to synagogue I usually just played hide-and-seek with the other kids amongst the heavy overcoats in the cloak room. (If you're curious what encroaching death smells like, it's the flat, grey musk of old people's wet coats hanging in a synagogue cloak room.) It took a long time for me to grow old enough to crack open Judaism's rich cache of legends, philosophical debates, and literal fanfiction based around Bible stories. Luckily I had *Final Fantasy VII* and *Mega*

Man Legends 2 for the PlayStation to blow my teenage mind until then.

As much as I loved my NES and SNES, I'm most nostalgic for the PlayStation. I was finally old enough to work part-time jobs, most of them awful, and my video game library fattened up considerably. I bought a PlayStation in 1998 alongside *Final Fantasy VII*, Squaresoft's genre-changing RPG. I recall trying to act too cool to care about *Final Fantasy VII*, but when advertisements for the follow-up to your favourite video game of all time show up in and on the city's buses, it's impossible not to be blown away. *Final Fantasy VII* was as cool as hell. It still is. Cloud is goddamn amazing, and by now he arguably has one of gaming's most recognizable character silhouettes.

My PlayStation was also the first game system that I had in my room. This was a life-changer. I'd always played video games on the living room TV, where my tastes were subject to commentary and critique. Locked in my room, playing on my own TV, though? I could consume as many weird RPG stories and crush over as many bishonen heroes as I wanted. Fun note, my "TV" was actually an old Commodore 64 monitor I rescued from my brother's room. He told me the set had no colour or volume, two problems I solved by fiddling with the monitor's colour and volume knobs. Take *that*, Columbo.

The monitor actually lacked a power button, so I had to turn it on and off by plugging and unplugging it. This repeated abuse eventually caused something in the monitor to go "pop," which was followed by the wispy scent of electrical smoke. Arrivederci, friend.

I quickly replaced the dead monitor with an actual TV so I could continue my private PlayStation sessions (and watch all the weird stuff that slithered out of the primordial muck of

Teletoon, Canada's animation station that was born around the same time.) But I got through most of *Final Fantasy VII* on that "fixed" monitor, in my *own* room, on a system I bought with *my* money, and on top of that, I was 17 or 18. I was independent. I was cool. I incessantly wore the shirt that came with the pre-order for *Mega Man X4*. My mind was open like a door, and I was primed to learn about the Lifestream, the Mountain Dew-coloured ribbon of bioenergy that fuels *Final Fantasy VII*'s story literally and figuratively.

When I started playing *Final Fantasy VII*, it hit me how similar its themes are to *Secret of Mana*'s. Shinra Inc., *Final Fantasy VII*'s world-dominating power company, (*cough*, weapons manufacturer,) is draining the planet of mako, which is essentially its lifeblood. Mako springs from the Lifestream, an undulating river of energy that flows through all things, gives them life, then collects their essence when they die. It's also a real handy-dandy source of electricity, which Shinra slurps up, processes, and sells with the help of Mako reactors, ugly structures that roost like steel vultures in cities, towns, and the wilderness.

Late-'90's SquareSoft was drunk on the PlayStation's exponential processing power over the SNES, to say nothing of all the extra data storage space courtesy of the new CD format. SquareSoft/Square Enix has always loved cinematic storytelling, and outside of the first time the studio attempted an actual theatrical movie release in 2001, it still renders and directs important story scenes with unmatched skill. Lord knows not every game by Square Enix is an epic tale guaranteed to hit you where you live, but I admire how much SquareSoft, Enix, and their amalgamated final form have contributed to the evolution of storytelling in video games.

Many religions and cultures believe everyone and everything carries a fragment of spiritual energy. Even Kabbalah, which teaches the more mystical side of Judaism, makes mention of souls reincarnating after being cleansed of sins. But for a lot of us, *Final Fantasy VII* was our first multimedia lecture about birth, death, rebirth, and humankind's place on the planet. It might be hard for a young person to understand these important story themes if they're presented in a book, but *Final Fantasy VII*'s combined visuals, text, and soundtrack (composed by returning Final Fantasy music master Nobuo Uematsu) help its message go down smoothly. Maybe a little *too* smoothly — Square Enix's corporate motto in the '90s may as well have been "Subtext is for Cowards." But after RPGs had spent so many quiet years in North America, it was good to see *Final Fantasy VII* getting in everyone's faces with its patchwork of inspirations from Kabbalah to James Lovelock's Gaia Hypothesis.

And those of us who never had a reason to think about the afterlife beyond Heaven and Hell, or indeed, never had a reason to think about the afterlife at all, found something special about the Lifestream, the lime-green tendrils that represent the planet's blood, spirit, and immune system. The Lifestream's double-sided nature makes it a fascinating study, too. Its comforting glow belays the great danger that comes with touching it, or worse, submerging yourself in it. Taking a dip in the physical manifestation of the planet's summed-up knowledge will overload your brain, short it out, and turn you into a gibbering, wide-eyed vegetable, as our hero Cloud eventually discovers during one of *Final Fantasy VII*'s darker story moments.

That's an exceptional occurrence: More commonly, people exposed to mako (which, again, is Lifestream that's been processed for commodification) suffer mako poisoning, which has side-effects not dissimilar from radiation poisoning in our world. Like nature itself, the Lifestream is the epitome of a neutral force that hurts as readily as it heals. It seeks to maintain the planet's equilibrium without bias.

Japanese games pull a lot of story material from its own traditions, cultures, and myths, but they're never shy about shoveling some Abrahamic symbolism in there, especially the kind that involves good/pure people becoming a blood sacrifice for the sake of saving humanity. (Spread arms and a white backdrop are optional but recommended.) As a teen, I found the mix compelling. It's rare for religions to cross-pollinate in the households of most nations, whereas Japan mixes Buddhist and Shinto traditions. That might be part of what encourages Japanese RPG developers to casually throw a pinch of Jesus into their works. Oh, and Hideaki Anno's 1995 anime masterpiece *Neon Genesis Evangelion* might be an inspiration.

That's a joke. *Evangelion* is still the font from which RPG themes and symbolism gush forth to this day, like a mother who cannot stop giving birth. How very Biblical. Let us titter sensibly.

It would be a few years before Anno's genre-shifting work was finally localized for English-speaking audiences, but Japanese RPG developers were seemingly infected by Anno's enthusiasm(?) about Kabbalah and Abrahamic mysticism and traditions. That energy seeped into *Final Fantasy VII*'s gritty story and its complicated characters, technically exposing us anime-deprived Westerners to the tough-to-digest themes in *Evangelion* before the official localization arrived. When snakebite is inevitable, sometimes it's good to dose yourself with the venom and build up that tolerance. What do you make of these themes if you're a kid who's been walled-in by a single "true" doctrine all your life? I'm asking for real. It must have been like taking drugs for the first time. Even I had no idea what the hell the Kabbalah was. I still don't have much of an idea, though I'm sure some Rabbi would tell me that's the point.

Late in the game, Cloud's band gets a stark lesson about where humans fit in amongst the Lifestream's inexorable flow. Story events direct *Final Fantasy VII*'s motley crew into the company of Bugenhagen, a kind-hearted wise man with sunglasses and a beard that tumbles down his body like an icy waterfall. Bugenhagen, an expert on the Lifestream, helps the gang work out Sephiroth's intention to summon the destructive magic known as "Meteor," which will subsequently slam a big-ass meteor into the planet. Thus the name. The planet, desperately wounded, will summon the Lifestream to repair the scarred land, and Sephiroth will absorb that power to become a deity.

Countless lives will die in the process — but not just from Meteor's impact. Bugenhagen suggests the Lifestream, which exists to protect and repair the planet, might determine humankind is a threat to the world's very existence and cull humans accordingly. For a brief, poignant moment we're left to wonder if Cloud's reward for saving the planet will be annihilation. Is it fair for regular people to be erased alongside the CEOs and corporate goons who actually put the machinations in place to drain mako? Maybe not, but everyone is complicit in relying on, using, and often wasting energy. That adds up in a well-populated world like *Final Fantasy VII*'s. If its planet is truly conscious, its Lifestream-powered immune system (engaged thanks to Aerith's sacrifice) will purge all threats alongside Sephiroth's pet Meteor.

Indeed, when the Lifestream arrives in the nick of time to break up Meteor after Sephiroth's death, we see a rendered cutscene of the Meteor being destroyed in a blinding flash of light before a vision of Aerith from the opening moments of *Final Fantasy VII* locks eyes with us and everything fades to black. Outside of post-credits stinger where an aged Red XIII runs alongside two adorable cubs to roar Lion King-style at the overgrown ruins of Cosmo Canyon's mako reactor, we have no idea what became of Cloud and his friends. Did the planet judge them unworthy to live, but spared Red XIII because of his connection to Cosmo Canyon? The last thing we hear is the laughter of children, insinuating that humanity was spared the Lifestream's wrath, but we never receive confirmation.

It took a while for me to warm up to *Final Fantasy VII*'s ending. I didn't like the suggestion that the planet might blot out humanity alongside Meteor. I wanted some kind of Happily Ever After. Even the deeply depressing *Final Fantasy VI* has an uplifting ending: Nearly everyone finds their peace and is ready to move on from their traumas. (Minus the sulky ninja Shadow, but what do you expect?)

I came around on *Final Fantasy VII*'s finale as I got older, though. It's a good example of a game's story asking that classic shonen question: Does humanity have a right to exist? What good are we for the planet, really? Despite their good deeds, Cloud and his friends are still subject to the Lifestream's judgement. What's the verdict? It's never spoken aloud, but that last sound of children laughing indicates we survived to some extent. Cloud, Tifa, Cid, Barret, that drip Vincent, Cait Sith, Yuffie, and of course Red XIII are presumably living as best they can in this brave new Shinra-free world.

It's a great conclusion for a great game that ultimately taught me to consider how life, death, and the planet are connected to each other. It's still fun to read and write about characters and monsters who are partitioned in the Christian idea of Heaven and Hell, (if we didn't have Catholicism's Seven Deadly Sins, half of the anime and game characters out there wouldn't have names,) but it's freeing to realize you can observe how people and nature function in life, then apply that knowledge to your own ideas about death and the afterlife. That's called world-building, baby, and you should do it as much as possible. It's good for you.

I continued to play PlayStation and question my own existence in equal parts. Now that my mind was cracked open, I was susceptible to the messages and questions put forth by another game: *Mega Man Legends 2*, released by Capcom in the year 2000. As a lifelong Mega Man fan, I can shoot on target, hop smoothly across platforms, and terrorize Robot Masters who are acting bad and wrong. But *Mega Man Legends 2* brought something new to the genre: Questions about the primal qualities that make us human, and whether or not those qualities are impeding our advancement as a species. Oh my God, it was hard enough to remember Snake Man's weakness, Capcom. (Needle Cannon.) Now we've got Descartes all up in the Flutter with Mega Man Volnutt and his family.

Mega Man Legends 2 is a great game. Mega Man Legends' canon is interesting, and the second installment gives us a hard look at what's become of the humans who once built and populated the world with marvelous robots. Its story is full of intrigue, and its characters are a joy to hang out with, especially the over-zealous Bonne air pirate family who tails Mega Man on his adventures. The PlayStation's infamous tank controls aren't everyone's cuppa tea, but they feel just right when you're taking on room-sized bosses. There's a reason us Mega Man fans have resolved to lie down and bang our heels on the floor until the promised *Mega Man Legends 3* is at least acknowledged again.

If you've made it this far into this book you're already familiar with how fond I am of wasting time talking about the Mega Man games' lore. But *Mega Man Legends*, and especially *Mega Man Legends 2* is driven by a narrative that still feels ahead of its time. As I write this, former Mega Man producer and Capcom employee Keiji Inafune is in exile for the Kickstarter Hindenburg that was 2016's *Mighty No. 9*, a platforming game that was supposed to be Mega Man's independent alternative. The *Mighty No. 9* gongshow can't be summarized in a paragraph; a breakdown would require a book of its own. In any case, the fiasco dented Inafune's reputation in a big way, and he's never really tried to clear the air about the whole mess. Inafune is currently hiding somewhere in his new home, Level-5 studios. He doesn't talk much, save for an incident in 2022 when he tried to hawk NFTs for some ugly characters who Definitely Weren't Inspired by *Mega Man X*'s Mavericks, No Sir. That pitch went over like a bird with two broken wings and it left a thin coat of slime on Inafune's already banged-up name.

I don't much like living in a world where one of the men responsible for designing my childhood hero turned out to be kind of scummy. It bums me out because Inafune was the world's biggest champion for the Mega Man Legends series, and that devotion and love for the property comes up to your armpits when you play *Mega Man Legends 2*. Inafune had a vision for the series that was never realized, and his departure from Capcom nuked the Mega Man franchise for years.

The Mega Man Legends series still hasn't been immortalized in a collection, unlike every other Mega Man series to date. (Except Mega Man Star Force for the Nintendo DS. Sorry, Omega-Xis stans.) It's as if Capcom got over its fear of acknowledging Mega Man, but still regards the Legends games as slightly radioactive. Capcom knows, as we all know deep in our genes, that the Mega Man Legends series is linked to Inafune's heart. If Capcom messes with the Legends games, it might be like waking a bear from torpor.

I can't profess to know what Keiji Inafune thinks. (Even though I just tried.) But as much as I'm disappointed in how things have gone for him, I respect that he chanelled his love for Legends into a story about mortality, free will, and entropy of the human body and soul. *Mega Man Legends 2* doesn't just feel like a dead end; it feels like a dead dream. I'm not saying we'll never see a Mega Man Legends game again, I'm just saying it takes a long time for life to adapt to a radioactive environment. I might be worm's meat before then. (Avenge me.)

The stories for *Mega Man Legends* and *Mega Man Legends 2* (as well as the delightful 1999 spinoff *The Misadventures of Tron Bonne*) aren't what you'd expect if the Blue Bomber first imprinted on you during the NES's heyday. There *is* a timeline to the Mega Man series that terminates with *Mega Man Legends 2*, a game with a story that goes beyond "Robot boy plus one robot dog saves the world from a mad scientist." The titular Mega Man of Mega Man Legends isn't quite a robot, but a highly specialized "carbon" — a hominid race that can modify itself with mechanical upgrades if so desired.

This iteration of Mega Man, who bears the surname "Volnutt," travels across a world "covered with endless water" with his family on their airship. Volnutt, his adoptive sister Roll, and their grandfather Barrell usually wind up on the few islands where carbons like themselves have built up their own unique societies. Mega Man Volnutt is a "Digger," which is a specialized adventurer who searches for energy "refractors" lingering in ancient ruins.

Mega Man Legends starts out with Mega Man Volnutt going on a standard dig to find a refractor to fuel their airship, the Flutter. Volnutt is subsequently chased by the ancient robot that's guarding the refractor, but manages to make a daring escape. It's standard adventure game stuff, albeit dressed up with low-poly anime charm that substitutes smeared 32-bit face textures for a bevy of facial expressions and emotions that fills Volnutt and his friends with an endearing Saturday morning anime quality. It's no chore to watch Mega Man Volnutt and Roll exchange verbal and physical blows with the Bonne family because the Legends games' aesthetics are still pleasing all these years later. But like all good adventure stories, the Mega Man Legends series carries a deep, dark secret. Don't forget, *Mega Man Legends* begins with Volnutt raiding a mysterious ruin while Roll spots him from the surface. Who made the ruins, though? Why are they all full of berserk robots?

The answer, again, touches on matters you wouldn't expect to find in a Mega Man game. I know the rest of the world is unlike myself, i.e. the rest of the world would rather stick their genitals into an ant hill than talk about the Mega Man series' timeline. But I yam who I yam, and I'm obligated to remind you that Mega Man Legends' "carbons" are far removed from the metal sons and soldiers of Dr. Light and Dr. Wily, but they're not unrelated. As the Mega Man games progressed and splintered into spin-offs, robots with human emotions (the Mega Man X and Mega Man Zero series) gradually fused into one cybernetic species (the Mega Man ZX series). Then, eons later, carbons populated a planet that was flooded by some unknown catastrophe that might be linked to events in the *Mega Man ZX* series.

By this point it's valid to ask "So who the hell *is* a human in the Mega Man series? Did the entirety of the human race mingle with machine parts and call it a day?" *Mega Man Legends 2* reveals there are indeed some pure flesh-and-blood humans in the world. Or just one, a near-immortal member of *homo sapiens* who is terribly lonely, jaded, and ready to erase himself alongside humanity's stored genetic code in order to give way to the next generation of hominids.

The last living human appears to be a kind-hearted young male with blonde hair that tumbles over his shoulders. Whatever else the human race's terminus thought and believed, his hair makes Zero's mane look like neglected Barbie doll hair.

When you watch the endgame cutscenes in *Mega Man Legends 2*, you can identify the question its development team wants us to consider. Is the life of a pure-blooded human like the Master more valuable than the lives of the carbons? After all, carbons are mere mortal constructs that toil upon the earth before returning to it. Humans are gods by comparison — immortal beings who've developed ways to free themselves of sickness and death. But to stay immortal, they must be confined in the sterile realm of "Elysium" which hovers just above the atmosphere like an ill moon.

Is a human still a human if they lose their mortality? What about if that endless life can only be enjoyed if said human stays contained in a hollowed-out egg suspended in space? Can a human evolve past the base instincts that keep us alive and propagating? *Should* we? Why are we so determined to reach perfection as a species? Was the Garden of Eden really *all that?* Is it worth giving up the human experience in exchange for all the knowledge in the world?

Mega Man Legends 2 gives us its answer when the Master descends from Elysium to observe the carbons he created and modified himself. The Master quickly falls ill while he's on the surface, demonstrating his inability to live amongst "his" people. Without Elysium's protection, the last human breaks down and dies on the soil of his ancestral home, granting him a little peace through the re-established link. I still wonder if some poor carbon child came across the Master's toga-swathed body and freaked out, because that's the kind of thought that just rises into my head, unbidden.

It's during this scene that Mega Man Volnutt, who is deep in the throes of an injury-induced flashback (O praise the favoured plot device of every writer!) remembers what he was created to do: He was, in part, a companion for the Master. He accompanied the Master on his last trip, who gave him the last humans' genetic code just before dying. The Master's last request for Mega Man is a biggie. He asks his companion to wipe out the humans' code and shut down the system Elysium existed for in the first place: To clone new humans and repopulate the surface. A process that involves wiping out the carbons who already live on the surface, presumably as test subjects for the planet's viability.

"For 3,000 years, I have been free from hardship and pain. A life of luxury and ease obeying my heart's desires," the

Master tells Volnutt as he fades. "Seeing these people, grateful for the simple joys of life, I wonder, was I truly happy?"

I played *Mega Man Legends 2* when I was 19; still young, but mature enough to start thinking a little harder about the mysteries of human consciousness. *Mega Man Legends 2* impressed upon me and I started applying the Master's line of thought to my everyday life. Who are we? *Why* are we? I gradually became more interested in philosophy, sociology, and the complexities that hinder communication and understanding between us as human beings. And once you open that door, you realize all that philosophy, sociology, and history winds back to one truth: We're deeply flawed and idiotic mammals who've barely evolved beyond the first apes to be spooked by fire. It's no surprise that sometimes we think and act irrationally. Lock a monkey in a china shop, filter in a bunch of noise and flashing lights, and observe how it deals with the stress. Five minutes later? No more china shop.

But it's these mortal quirks that fascinated the Master in the first place. The carbons in *Mega Man Legends 2* aren't human by blood, but it's enough that the Master still remembered how humans acted 3,000 years ago. He clearly thought enough of our imperfections that he not only echoed them in his own creations, but he chose to die amongst those creations — despite the possibility of his hyper-evolved body being poked at by some carbon kid armed with a stick.

Mega Man Legends 2 taught me something distressing about myself: I like people. No matter how many times we regress and give in to that easily-panicked, animalistic side of ourselves, there's always the side that's instinctively kind and curious. We're fully capable of building a better world — we've been in space, for the luvva God! — and we're more than clever enough to band together to get ourselves out of this climate mess we've lodged ourselves in. Heck, we have the collective brainpower to solve anything, do anything, build anything. But we'd rather burn that money and energy on endless wars that turn countries of sand and rubble into more sand and more rubble. It's easy to understand why Keiji Inafune used *Mega Man Legends 2* to ask one of those anime plot cliches that are no less poignant for their overuse: After all the damage we've done, is it time for humans to step back from our dominant role on Earth and let new forms of life succeed us?

Maybe we need a good shepherd like *Mega Man Legends 2*'s Master. It seems as long as we non-Elysian humans lack someone to guide us, we're destined to flail and hurt ourselves like confused Pokémon. But to paraphrase astronomer Carl Sagan, there's no sign in the wide, wide universe that anyone is coming to save us from ourselves. We're doughy and undercooked as far as sentient life goes, but all we have is each other. And video games. And the stories those games tell. And the fanfiction sins that follow those game stories the same way bastard children follow a moonlit fling.

Notes

McFerran, Damien (2010). *How Colecovision Became the King of Kong*. Nintendo Life.

Sheff, David (1999). *Game Over: Press Start to Continue: The maturing of Mario*. Cyberactive Media Group.

Caruso, Norman (2016). *Nintendo's Battle Against Video Game Rentals*. Gaming Historian.

Oxford, David (2018). *Howard Phillips Speaks on Dragon Quest's Initial Performance and Nintendo Power Giveaway*. Old School Gamer Magazine.

Kishi (2017). *Gaming computers of Japan: the NEC PC-8800 series*. Retronauts.

McFerran, Damien (2025). *Why Do Americans Keep Ignoring European Gaming History?* Time Extension.

David, Margaret (2023). *Why Dragon Quest Has Always Been So Much More Popular in Japan.* Den of Geek.

Eisenbeis, Richard (2025). *Creating a Classic JRPG in the Modern Era: An Interview with Final Fantasy Creator Hironobu Sakaguchi.* Anime News Network.

Nob (1994). *Interview with Yusuke Hirata.* EGM Magazine no. 63.

Clark, Brian (2017). *25 Years Since The Release Of Final Fantasy VI – Looking Back At The Passion.* Famitsu / One Million Power.

Bjarneby, Tobias., Szczepaniak, John. (2022.) *The Late Rieko Kodama on Phantasy Star, Skies of Arcadia, and Challenging Stereotypes.* LEVEL Magazine / Time Extension.

Kikuta, Hiroki (2014). Reddit AMA ("Ask Me Anything").

Schaufelberger, Fredrik. Killer Bob (2006 / 2015) *Interview with Hiromichi Tanaka and Koichi Ishii.* LEVEL Magazine / Chrono Compendium.

Kincaid, Chris (2021). *Unhappily Ever After: The Endings of Japanese Fairy Tales.* Japan Powered.

Jackson, Gita (2018). *It Used to Be Perilous to Write Fanfiction.* Kotaku.

Leone, Matt (2017). *Final Fantasy 7: An Oral History.* Polygon.
Walker, Ian (2020). *Moon Designer Credits Toby Fox with Motivating Western Release.* Kotaku.

Copp, Jay (1997). *The Nagasaki Martyrs.* Catholic Culture.

Acknowledgements

Most acknowledgement pages start with some variation of the idiom "No man is an island," because it's the truth. Good writers are Katamaris that collect stories, experiences, and friends as they roll along according to the whims of a drunken god. If you're not hip enough to understand a Katamari reference, just picture a wet, basketball-sized wad of chewed gum rolling across a mall parking lot. I am the gum, and the stories are the dirt, trash, and used syringes I pick up along the way.

That means it's time to belt out some thank-yous, so lettuce do this.

I hereby pledge to drain half my blood and mail it to the Mechadrake crew, most of whomst have stuck by me since the aughts — or sooner. Thank you for all the times you've lifted me on your shoulders and carried me without complaint across the mighty deserts of No Confidence and No Money. The rest of my blood goes to the Axe of the Blood God crew and community, especially Kat Bailey, Eric Van Allen, Victor

Hunter, and Mike Williams who is forever Sharlayan Dropouts alumni.

Not a whole lot of blood left to give away, so I'd like to mail my drained viscera to my Pa and Ma, my brothers, and the people who taught me and flogged me back into obedience whenever my writing got stupid: Jeremy Parish, John Davison, Jason Wilson, and Caty Williams.

My heart goes to my husband of 20-summat years, David Oxford, and the animals that have been in and out of my life.

My skin obviously goes to Retro Game Books, who took a chance on this diary of sin in the first place. Shout out to Brian Riggsbee and Justin Severson for their thorough edits of my initial word-jumble. You *can* vomit on a page and publish it, but it's not always the best idea in the universe. I understand that now.

Thank You for Reading ! !

Presented by
Nadia

www.ingramcontent.com/pod-product-compliance
Lightning Source LLC
Chambersburg PA
CBHW071345230926
51846CB00002B/455
* 9 7 8 1 9 6 6 0 0 9 0 3 0 *